Getting the Best Out of Yourself and Others

Also available from Harper & Row by Buck Rodgers

THE IBM WAY

Getting the Best Out of Yourself and Others

By BUCK RODGERS
with Irv Levey

1817

Harper & Row, Publishers, New York

Cambridge, Philadelphia, San Francisco, Washington
London, Mexico City, São Paulo, Singapore, Sydney

This book is dedicated to
Helen and Irene,
for their understanding,
patience, and motivation

FIRST EDITION

Designer: Laura Hough
Copy editor: Marjorie Horvitz

Library of Congress Cataloging-in-Publication Data
Rodgers, F. G. (Francis G.)
    Getting the best out of yourself and others.
    1. Employee motivation. 2. Achievement motivation. 3. Performance. 4. Employee assistance programs.
I. Levey, Irv. II. Title.
HF5549.5.M63R63 1987   658.3'14   86-46125
ISBN 0-06-015670-8

87 88 89 90 91 RRD 10 9 8 7 6 5 4 3 2 1

CONTENTS

CONTENTS

CONTENTS

ix

ACKNOWLEDGMENTS

Special thanks to Christy Rodgers Smith and Mark Levey: Christy, for her probing questions, thoughtful criticisms, and insightful contributions; Mark, for keeping our word processors humming day after day throughout the writing of this book and for tenaciously insisting that the rules of grammar and punctuation be considered allies. Thanks, too, to our editor, Hugh Van Dusen, for his wise and gentle guidance.

1

Getting Ready
for the Good Times

W e live in a time of paradox, contradiction, opportunity, and above all change. To the fearful, change is threatening because they worry that things may get worse. To the hopeful, change is encouraging because they feel things may get better. To those who have confidence in themselves, change is a stimulus because they believe one person can make a difference and influence what goes on around them. These people are the doers and the motivators.

No matter who you are—CEO of a big company or independent business person; marketing representative or purchasing agent; homemaker or engineer; student or lawyer—there are exciting possibilities ahead. If you are willing to assume responsibility and accountability and are motivated to enhance your own capabilities and performance, there's no limit to what you can achieve.

In spite of all the trouble spots in the world today, there's plenty to be optimistic about as we close out the 1980s. We're not involved in any war, and inflation, unemployment, and interest rates are down and will hopefully continue to stay in the reasonable range. The key is never to lose sight of the fact that each of us can make a difference and affect the quality of our lives and of those around us.

THE NEED FOR TOP PERFORMERS

I predict that the individuals and companies that will be successful in the '90s and beyond are those willing to adopt the kind of values, work ethics, and resolve that propelled this nation to greatness. They will demand excellence of themselves, and will not tolerate much less from others.

Not everyone agrees with me: not everyone is ready for the changing times. At a recent meeting, I was sharing these thoughts with a group of business people, and one interrupted. "Come on, Buck," he said, "you've spent too much time with IBM. You and they have excellence on the brain, but IBM's an anomaly. In the real world, excellence is something you read about and maybe talk about. It doesn't creep into very many real-life situations, though." Each time I'm confronted with that attitude, I want to explode or cry, because it's a point of view that got us into a lot of trouble during the last three decades, and it's obviously hard to shake off.

THE SEEDS OF MEDIOCRITY

For too many years, we have been floating listlessly in a sea of mediocrity. We sat on its beaches and became soft and bloated. Mediocrity is an enemy that must not be ignored. A manifestation of complacency and lethargy, it's been around so long that too many of us have gotten used to it. Some of our younger people have lived with it all their lives.

It probably started in the '60s, and we suffer still. For more than two decades, it seemed we lost our way. Vietnam unraveled us, and every part of our society suffered. Government, business, industry, the educational system, and families seemed to break down. Right and wrong became blurred,

4

along with our moral standards and our attitudes at home and in the workplace. Many declared that small is beautiful and less is more; but we settled for less quality, less service, less courtesy, less thoughtfulness. Some companies that attempted to maintain their level of excellence were considered by many to be part of an insensitive, antiquated establishment.

While some of our leaders were further damaging the image of the establishment by playing Watergate—a drama that might have been written, directed, and cast by Woody Allen—double-digit inflation complicated, confused, and weakened the marketplace.

We were continually distracted throughout the '70s by the endless Israeli-Arab conflict; Khomeini humiliated us by taking U.S. hostages; Middle East terrorists murdered our Marines. We poured money into the Third World and they hated us. When OPEC punished us with their oil embargo, it appeared that the mobile lifestyle that was second nature to us was quickly coming to an end.

All our bad times weren't caused by outsiders who wanted to undo us. Some of our greatest problems have been self-inflicted. We forgot who we were; we seemed to lose our belief in ourselves, our power to shape and control events—our magic.

OUR JAPANESE LESSON

The United States has been the world's leading producer of agricultural and industrial products for over a hundred years. We have been the land of the entrepreneurs, the innovators, and the inventors. The whole world knew that, but now our pride, like our pocketbooks, has been battered and bruised by the Japanese, who demonstrated that they can be more industrious than we and more ingenious. That really hurts. Hell, we invented those words! Now countries we never considered capable of competing with us (especially at home) are biting at our heels. Korea, Hong Kong, Taiwan. The Hyundai! Of course, it's our own fault. We can't blame the foreign entrepreneur or the industrialist for moving into marketplaces we neglected, with products that are often superior to ours and less expensive.

We know what happened. While the Japanese industrialists set their sights on American markets, American industrialists had their eyes glued on their short-term profit-and-loss statements. The Japanese researched, planned, and invested. The Americans were overly cautious about R & D, and failed to make meaningful commitments to education and training, responding to every economic change by turning these programs on and off, like a spigot. They were more interested in bringing as much money as possible down to the bottom line than in investing wisely in the future. Financial and security analysts pressured even good management into shortening its focus and losing long-term perspectives. The Japanese not only copied and improved on our management styles, they also listened to their workers; and they listened to the American consumer and acted on what they heard. They courted our consumers, who ignored our home-grown products.

The big thing the Japanese had going for them was their high expectations, their commitment to success. They made up their mind to outperform us, and did. They nurtured the conditions necessary to evoke that superior performance, and motivated their work force to strive for excellence and productivity. Their resolve to produce the best was comparable to our own resolve during World War II, when government, industry, business, and the individual worker were proud to work their tails off for the "war effort."

WE SEEM TO HAVE LOST
OUR MAGIC

I worked in a company that never forgot its commitment to excellence, and part of my job was to make sure that commitment was kept alive—in spite of Vietnam, Watergate, inflation, or oil embargoes. So it's difficult for me to be sympathetic to companies that became smug, soft, and even lazy. Too many people who were paid to manage companies or departments in companies became involved in personal struggles to the detriment of those who relied on them; they played internal, unprofitable games, with title, status, and power as their targets. Unfortunately for some of them, they were building themselves secure cabins on sinking ships.

Overly cautious leadership and unimaginative management aren't the only causes of our less than vibrant business and industrial environment. True, they fail to encourage creativity or motivate their people to perform more productively; but the worker and his organizations also contribute their share to the mediocrity we find too often in American business.

While the rest of the world seemed hell-bent on becoming more productive, much of our work force dropped the work ethic as though it were something to be ashamed of. Instead of striving for a superior performance, their goal was more pay and less work. Management accepted this condition without much of a fight, often giving in to demands that lowered the quality of products and services and increased prices.

Some unions and employee associations have rejected programs that would reward their members for increased productivity. I mean cash incentives, trips, and merchandise.

7

They rejected meritocracy, a system of pay for performance, in favor of across-the-board raises regardless of the quality or quantity of work done. The companies that pressed for incentives and performance increases were accused of trying to encourage competition among employees. Incredibly, in a country that flourished under the free enterprise system, competition in the workplace became feared and discouraged.

Bad management often alienates its people by being insensitive and unappreciative. In addition, employee associations and unions protect their members regardless of the quality of their work or attitude. The only ones who benefit are employees who don't deserve to hold on to their position. Walk through the halls of almost any good-sized company and see the result of this kind of employment relationship: phones ring unanswered on desks whose occupants are late for work or called in sick or are socializing with other people, interfering with their work.

Indeed, both management and labor have contributed to poor quality, bad service, and high prices; but their time is running out. In order for any company to survive the competitive pressure, excellence in service and quality of product must be a way of life.

THE CUSTOMER CRIES FOUL
AND BUSINESS BEGINS TO LISTEN

Poorly managed and weakly staffed businesses will not make it in the 1990s. The companies that flourish will be the ones that welcome and reward people who are capable, ambitious, energized; they will get rid of those who put out the minimum effort and bring down their colleagues with their negativism and disinterest. I proclaim it's time to get moving, because those who fail to prepare themselves for this exciting turnabout in American business will miss out on the opportunity of a lifetime.

At last, the business community is awakening to the fact that it desperately needs superior performers. It settled for less for too long. Shoddy work, negative attitudes, and sloppy work habits are becoming unacceptable. The American consumers who accepted inferior products and services from these mediocre companies, as though they had no recourse, are also waking up, thanks to our Japanese competitors. They will no longer accept poor service or pay outrageous prices for inferior products. The consumer's message to American business is: *"Clean up your act! You shoved inferior quality and rotten service on us long enough. If you want our business, you'd better raise your sights; you'd better listen to us; you'd better provide value."*

GOOD NEWS FOR THE WILD DUCKS

American business *is* beginning to listen. That's good news for all of us, but it's terrific news for those in the workplace, from entry level positions to operating officers, who recognize the change as a great opportunity and are motivated to take advantage of it.

More now than ever before, business and industry recognize the frightening cost of weak or misguided leadership and an unmotivated work force. They sense the urgency to identify and develop strong leaders and dedicated workers. Product quality, along with listening to your people, are the marks of success.

Smart business now knows that to withstand the fierce competition of the international business community, it must seek out, embrace, and nurture the innovators, the corporate entrepreneurs, and the high-level producers. That means a

9

major shift in attitude. For years, there has been what amounts to a conspiracy by big business against what IBM called the "wild ducks," talented people who don't fit the company's mold or job descriptions. Perceiving them as unpredictable and more difficult to supervise than the average employee, management has gone to great lengths to avoid the "wild ducks." Behavioral scientists have been commissioned to design applicant tests that carefully screen out exceptional people—the exceptionally good along with the exceptionally bad. "Engineered mediocrity," someone called it. This system has created a comfortable, even serene environment for a lot of people, with nobody rocking the boat or asking off-the-wall questions or blue-skying, when he could be writing benign reports and unnecessary analyses.

A company that effectively fences out creative people loses not only their ideas but also the stimulation they usually bring to every discussion and situation. The policies and the tests that help foster this age of mediocrity are guaranteed to reduce the level of excitement and enthusiasm in a company.

Thank goodness, times are changing. I know that every day, *American companies are waking up to the fact that they must inject excitement, enthusiasm, and creativity into their businesses.* The once feared and ignored wild duck is certain to become a sought-after prize.

WE HAVE THE POTENTIAL—WE NEED THE MOTIVATION

Our problem in the immediate future will be not the lack of opportunities for the really motivated, but the lack of motivated people ready and able to take advantage of the opportunities. There's no shortage, right now, of people who have intelligence and ability for success—even spectacular success

10

—but few of them perform at the superior level I'm talking about. Some of it is understandable. There's been too little *healthy* pressure put on most people to get them to stretch for their potential. There's been pressure, all right, but the wrong kind. It comes from frightened supervisors, who worry more about protecting their turf and their position than about getting the best out of their people or themselves. Then there's the kind of pressure that's manufactured by a management obsessed with squeezing every last penny a share out of a budget already wrung dry at the expense of the company's future growth.

It's tough to be "up" and motivated in poorly managed companies. It's unfortunate that so many potentially superior performers have their enthusiasm and desire squeezed out of them by unmotivated supervisors, inept managers, and uninvolved executives. It's a great loss to the business world when good people hang on to unrewarding jobs as though they love them, scared to death they'll end up out of work. Before long, they become disillusioned and take on the ways of those who had no ambition to start with. Of course, it's the responsibility of the company to do everything it can to provide the very best working environment for its employees; but no one impacts the environment as much as the people in it.

As often as not, the pressures the employee brings to work are more crippling than those that confront him or her on the job.

The stressful situations that even the average person has to cope with can be mind boggling. If you're like many of the people I meet, it's a miracle that you're doing as well as you are, considering the circumstances.

The majority of married couples today work. It certainly makes it easier to pay bills and buy things, but it's sure to bring extra stress to your relationship. There's the hassle of who's responsible for what household chores, coordinating vacation times, potential career jealousies, not to mention how each paycheck figures into the family budget.

The stress factor is compounded when you add children into the equation, especially for women. Women must consider the biological time clock when they set career goals. From there, balancing the roles of wife, mother, and career woman can only be achieved with the help of a supporting and understanding spouse.

Working couples and single parents must address the problems of latch-key child raising. Children face the questions of drugs, sex, peer pressure, and competition in school at an earlier age than before. Establishing lines of communication has always been a challenge to every parent, but the child who comes home to an empty house and no one to talk to is a sad commentary on today's society.

THE PRESSURE TO PERFORM

For all of us, at times, the pressure to perform is tremendous. It doesn't matter what your occupation is or how successful you may be; you feel the strain—the strain of competition and expectations. You feel it in all the roles you play and in your relationships. You may worry about earning a living, being an effective parent, your marriage, being a caring friend.

Bungling bosses, unhappy mates, and children who seem to be slipping away cause plenty of grief, but a lot of the burden we carry to work is self-inflicted: created out of fears, misperceptions, and low self-esteem. We blame ourselves, then go to our job and try to cope with the work load. No wonder so many of us, one way or another, seem to be reaching out for help, recognition, understanding, and peace of mind.

Let's face the hard facts: No matter how intense the pressure, no matter what the situation, you have to roll out of bed every morning and you have to perform. Like it or not, the quality of that performance depends on you. You may think that you're doing a pretty good job, especially considering the circumstances, but I know you can do a whole lot better. I say that with complete conviction, because for the past thirty-five years, I've been helping people to improve their performance and productivity. True, I work in a big-business milieu, but what I've learned and what I teach about motivating yourself and others—about being effective, influential, and successful— can help you reach any goal, in or out of business. It can help you order your priorities, improve your relationships, project the right image. For certain, what I'm "selling" can help anyone escape the bland mediocrity that has trapped so many of us at work and at home.

You have to believe this: *Mediocrity is in trouble!* It's up to all of us to keep it there and not accept it as a way of life. You must do what I and others have done. Reject mediocrity like the plague, eliminate it from your life whenever you can. *The first thing you must do toward that end is to raise the level of your own performance and encourage those you care about or work with to do the same.* It won't take long to get started —only about as long as it will take you to read this book.

ABOUT PERFORMING AND THE GREAT PERFORMANCE

I want to talk first about performance in general, then about specifics. The word "performance" most often conjures up an image of a theatrical or sports event. When we think of great performers, names like Leontyne Price, Itzhak Perlman, Katharine Hepburn, Larry Bird, and Jack Nicklaus come to mind. But most performers aren't standing in a spotlight, facing their "customers." The fact is, we're all performers.

13

It doesn't matter what you do for a living or if you work at all; whenever you charge yourself up, put a smile on your face—or a scowl—and attempt to influence the behavior or attitude of someone else, you're performing. You may be trying to influence your kids to behave or your spouse to save money or your clients to spend money. You may be trying to make someone laugh or cry or lower his prices or exceed her sales quota. It doesn't matter. If you're *doing* anything at all, you're performing whether you're conscious of it or not; and the better you do it, the more effective and successful you're certain to be.

For some people, the idea of performing for the purpose of influencing someone else evokes a negative connotation. It shouldn't. There's certainly nothing wrong with trying to "get your way"—that is, so long as your way isn't deviously manipulative and doesn't take unfair advantage of someone else. Since we all started performing for attention, comfort, needs, and power when we were infants, it's a wonder that we're not better at it as adults.

There's no doubt in my mind that the most successful of us, professionally and privately, are the best performers. I know that the demand on us to improve our performance will surely increase. What does it take for you or anyone—executive, salesperson, or parent—to be a top-notch performer? I'll discuss these elements as we get into this book, but here are some of the success factors in a nutshell:

- You need to be on good terms with yourself.
- You must be motivated—a catalyst, a self-starter.
- You must know what you want to accomplish.
- You must have the necessary tools and information to achieve your goal.

14

- You must have the skills to deliver your material or make your case in the most influential way possible.
- You need an interested audience: an individual or a group that can somehow benefit or derive pleasure from your performance.
- You must be able to establish with that audience a relationship that is sensitive and responsive to both its needs and yours.
- You must be fine-tuned to pick up others' reactions to you, not only during your performance but after it.

All these things, along with *poise, self-confidence,* and *integrity,* are imperative to a superior performance and would assure you of being a decent performer, maybe a good one, but it takes even more to make the performer great.

Great performances are filled with intense, concentrated energy. I don't mean nervous hyperenergy, but the kind that exudes passion, caring, enthusiasm, and joy. It's manifested in a quiet ballad sung by Frank Sinatra and in the controlled hysterical rock of Tina Turner. It's as vital to a monologue by Bill Cosby as it is to a soliloquy by Sir Laurence Olivier. It's an energy that's captivating, hypnotizing, and contagious.

The show-business analogy helps make my point; but please understand that you don't need a stage or a stadium to accomplish what I'm talking about. It can happen when you're making a presentation to a board of directors or a prospective customer. It can happen as you try to instill the love of God in a wayward child. It can happen anytime you're dealing with other people—trying to influence them, motivate them, incite them, change them, and inspire them.

A great performance occurs when all the factors I mentioned fall in place, as if effortlessly and naturally: the self-

15

worth, the knowledge, the skill, the rapport, the sensitivity, the concentration, and the energy. When it all comes together, the performer—and that can be any of us—experiences an incredible sense of well-being and accomplishment . . . sometimes even of ecstasy.

If this were the only reward for the superior performer, it would be worth the struggle to become one. Of course, there are other rewards: career enhancement; money and what it buys; respect and recognition from others, as well as from yourself.

It is worth the effort.

2

The First Steps
Toward a Superior
Performance

A lmost every day of the week, I meet with a different group of people to help solve some of the problems that will be dealt with in this book. It doesn't matter what the business or industry is—electronics, communications, banking, insurance, real estate, retailing, manufacturing, or education—or what level of the organizational chart I'm working with; the meeting usually starts off with the question: "How can we increase revenues and productivity without disproportionately increasing incremental costs?" Even more to the point: "How can we dramatically improve the performance of this company?" Basically, it's the same question we as individuals must answer if we hope to become the very best we can. "How can I improve my performance?" Here's what I tell them.

YOU MUST ARTICULATE YOUR VALUES AND BELIEFS

This seems so simple and obvious that you might want to slide over it, but please don't. Some may feel that words like "values" and "beliefs" are inappropriate in a book that deals with ambition, productivity, and bottom lines, but they are two major factors that separate the truly superior performers from the average or mediocre.

I tell every company I work with: *"The first thing you must do to become a great organization is spell out in writing your beliefs and purpose. Write a credo that will be a behavioral guide to every person in your company, from entry level positions to CEO."* This creed, once thought out and formalized, should become as much a part of a company's operation as its product, service, or policies.

Tom Watson, Sr., of IBM put his creed to paper in 1914 before he hired the company's first employees. He wanted them to know before they accepted a job just what kind of company he intended to build. He also wanted them to know that if they *demonstrated* a set of values that were incompatible with his, they'd be fired. He and his son Tom, Jr., and every leader who followed them believed that the incredible success of IBM was built on the few words he wrote down and distributed to each employee he hired:

> *One, the individual must be respected. Two, the customer must be given the best possible service. Three, excellence and superior performance must be pursued.*

I don't know how long it took Watson to compose those words, but they are still in force—and are the heart of "IBM's Business Conduct Guidelines," which is distributed to every employee once a year and is considered required reading.

I firmly believe that a company must continuously articulate its values and beliefs to its employees in the most simple, straightforward terms—at meetings and conferences, in memos, newsletters, and house organs, in informal conversations, and at performance appraisals. These principles should be focused on in recruiting, training, and planning programs.

The payoff, of course, is measured in the positive effect those published beliefs have on the company's personnel, its policies, and its customer and community relationships.

A COMPANY CULTURE

When a set of values such as Watson's is adopted for a company, it humanizes that organization by setting the tone for the way people in the organization do business. It's also the basis for a company's culture. I know that some people are frightened by the idea of a "company culture." They associate the words with Big Brother, a mandated social structure, and brainwashing; but that's baloney. The culture is simply a manifestation of the common interests of the company's personnel, regardless of their titles or responsibilities. In companies wise enough to put a code of behavior in place, the culture usually expresses mutual respect for talent, intelligence, and hard work. People who care about their work help everyone in the company. Besides, when a company publishes its beliefs and its code of behavior and ethics, it draws people whose personal values are at least compatible with theirs. Don't get the mistaken idea that with the publication of such values a company is less attractive to the entrepreneur. There is no conflict of interests in being a corporate entrepreneur or a free creative spirit and having to function within a prescribed operational philosophy.

VALUES VS. BEHAVIOR

What about individuals: Does it do them any good to take a conscious look at their values and set guidelines for their own behavior? Of course it does. I'm convinced that a great deal of

21

the stress people experience is caused by the conflict between their true values and their behavior. The more they are in touch with their beliefs, the greater their chance of avoiding unpleasant stress.

Here's an enlightening exercise: On one sheet of paper make a list of your values in order of importance—those ideals, beliefs, and even people you deem influential in your life. Put the list away, and the next day, on another paper, record the way you spend your time and energy. List activities in order of the time they consume. Now compare the two lists: The areas of stress and conflict will leap off the pages.

A few years ago, I met an Australian psychiatrist who had just completed an experiment to make this same point. He said he "contracted" for three prostitutes to come to his office. When they showed up, he paid their fee and told them to disrobe. Without any hesitation they began to undress, then he stopped them.

"Put your clothes on," he said. "What I really want to do is hypnotize the three of you, give you two or three very simple instructions, and see if you can follow them."

After a few moments' hesitation, they agreed. The trance state was swiftly achieved, and the prostitutes began to follow the doctor's orders. First they hopped around the office like kangaroos; then they stood on one leg without moving a muscle.

Then he said, "Okay, ladies, here's a hundred dollars for each of you; now please disrobe."

They wouldn't do it! According to this doctor, people will not do anything under hypnosis that offends their true values. While they were in this altered state of consciousness, he was dealing with their subconscious minds, the repositories of their true values. Unfortunately, when we're awake and making conscious decisions, we bury some of our most precious values.

Your performance is certain to improve when you are really in touch with your values. The more we consider them as an important factor in our decisions and our actions, the less apt we'll be to behave in a way that causes us discomfort and stress.

The successful head of a large sales organization told me this story: "When I began my sales career, I had a three-state territory, selling paper products for a fairly large manufacturer. Although I loved selling and enjoyed traveling, it was tough going for me. It wasn't the work or the pay; it was the company's attitude toward their field people that began to raise doubts in my mind. Management 'rode herd' with a vengeance and set policies that I thought showed nothing but suspicion and contempt. For example, we were required to submit to our district manager an *hourly* call report that detailed everything except maybe bathroom time. Well, one Saturday morning, I received a phone call from our national sales manager. My boss was moving to the main office, and I was being promoted to district manager. It meant a substantial raise, a company car, and travel expenses—things I didn't get as a rep. After he told me all the good things that were coming my way, he suggested we meet to go over the reports I would have to monitor, the problem reps I'd be responsible for, and so forth. As he spoke, I felt a deep sense of discomfort, which quickly turned to sadness. It was then that I finally realized I had lived too long in this autocratic environment.

"My wife entered the room just as I hung up the phone, and could see that I was disturbed.

" 'Was that your boss?'

" 'Yes.'

" 'I can tell it was bad news. Were you fired?'

" 'Worse.'

" 'What could be worse?' She was almost in tears.

23

" 'I was promoted.'

"When I sorted out my feelings, I felt crushed because the people whom I had so little respect for thought I was one of them—they believed I could behave in a way that would fit their managerial requirements."

"How did you handle the promotion?" I asked him.

"I concluded that I couldn't change things in that company, so I made two phone calls. The first was to my sales manager, who accepted my resignation by slamming the phone in my ear. The second call was to our baby-sitter, so my wife and I could go to our favorite restaurant and celebrate our very important commitment to doing what we knew was right."

YOU MUST DEMONSTRATE THE VALUES YOU PROFESS

To be a superior performer—company or individual—you must have integrity. People must know what to expect of you. Once you make a commitment to a belief, a person, or a task, it's imperative that you honor it down to the smallest detail.

One reason for so much cynicism in American business is the gap between what is promised and what is delivered. Through the media and their sales organizations, companies promise us the very best—products made of the best materials, produced by the most skillful workers, sold at prices that make them the best value, and serviced by the happiest, most caring people in the world. People don't believe most companies' advertising or salespersons' promises. They don't expect the product that's delivered to look as good as it appears in magazines, commercials, or brochures. They're surprised if the product survives the warranty; and they're amazed if they're served with the courtesy, attention, and enthusiasm promised when they're being wooed by marketing.

There are exceptions, companies that became great because they deliver what they promise. They have integrity. McDonald's is one. The stores and sandwiches look exactly as they do in the commercials. The people behind the counter are clean and friendly. The rest rooms are inspected and cleaned frequently. Neiman-Marcus became one of the most successful retailers in America because it delivered to the customer what it promised: guaranteed satisfaction. The company I know most about, IBM, is the personification of the word "integrity." It's an organization made up of about 400,000 individuals who know that their career depends on their own ability to produce and meet commitments. IBMers who don't deliver what they promise or what IBM promises won't be IBMers very long.

We all know that you don't have to have integrity to make a lot of money—at least, not in the short run; but those who hope to be successful over the long term need the cooperation, loyalty, and respect of others. You'd better begin now to build open, honest relationships. The future will favor people of integrity—those doers who keep their promises, meet their commitments, deliver value, and strive for excellence.

A MATTER OF RESPECT

The one single action management can take to increase the company's productivity is to communicate the following to employees: "From this moment on, every policy that we put in place will demonstrate our respect for you, our customers, and the company's ownership. With your help, we will examine those policies, programs, and attitudes now in force, and correct any that shows disrespect or takes unfair advantage of anyone."

Disrespect for the individual may be the costliest long-term error a company can make! Respect, on the other hand, is one of the greatest motivators for a superior performance.

The employee who comes to work believing that he is not respected by his company or his boss cannot consistently give a superior performance. *People work best when they feel good about themselves; and they do not feel good about themselves if they feel abused, taken advantage of, ignored, or disliked.*

IT STARTS WITH SELF-RESPECT

If every person really felt good about himself, appreciated his worth, recognized his strengths, handled his weaknesses with objectivity, understood that guilt and depression are acts of self-abuse; if every person respected himself as he wishes others to respect him, there would be little need for motivational books.

I don't pretend to be a psychologist—not even an amateur psychologist—but I've worked with thousands of people, most of whom professed ambition, motivation, and the willingness to learn and work. I'm convinced that all of them were anxious to succeed. All had personal goals and aspirations, none expected a free ride, but not all succeeded or reached their full potential. Those who did had a healthy, realistic, and understanding opinion of themselves. Most of those who failed, I believe, failed themselves first.

Each of us has to find the key to our own heart and spirit if we are going to attain a success worth achieving—that is, a success that gives us pleasure, adds to our self-worth, and brings us peace of mind.

Someone once said, "As a man thinketh, so is he." What we think, what we believe, and what we feel affect the quality of our lives and the level of our performances more than any other factors. Over the years, I developed a belief system that has helped me deal with almost any situation that's confronted me. It reflects the influence of such people as Tom Watson, Jr., Bishop Fulton J. Sheen, and my father. It's pretty basic stuff, but it has a lot more to do with my business success, the quality of my life, and the way I perform than do my astrology charts, biorhythms, or luck.

I share these beliefs with you in hope that they may help you achieve greater satisfaction in your professional and personal life.

1. You were created to enjoy the blessings of life. You have to believe that! Do everything possible to convince yourself it's so. You mustn't let anyone or any circumstance or experience convince you that you're unworthy of happiness.

You can't enjoy the blessings of life at home or at work if you are continuously looking behind you, wishing you had done things differently, feeling guilty for actions that don't even deserve a place in your memory. You can't enjoy your life if you're so frightened of the future that your preoccupation with it causes you to stumble blindly through the present.

Fifty years ago, Jacob Tarshish (an Ohio philosopher and theologian) told his radio audience: "Say this to yourself each morning: 'This is the only day I have to live. Yesterday is gone and, no matter how I try, I cannot change it. Tomorrow is not yet here, nor do I know if it will ever come. Therefore, let me make the most of today.' " This idea has been expressed many ways, and you may want to pass it off as sort of hokey homespun philosophy; but I never met a truly happy person who thinks it's trite.

Indeed, we were created to enjoy the blessings of life. Most of us knew that when we were little kids; we lived each day without wallowing in the misfortunes of the past and had no time during that day to worry about the dangers of the future. Those who outgrew the child in them may long for those wondrous days. I think it's important to keep the child in us alive and healthy. I don't mean that as an exercise in nostalgia. I mean we should be as receptive as a child to the beauty and excitement of discovery, allow our creative energy to flow without embarrassment, welcome innocent thoughts and fight off cynicism.

I don't shut out my past, but I have what I consider a selective memory. I pick and choose which memories I'll draw from my memory bank, and I have chosen those that make me feel good. Of course, I haven't total control over these things, but since I can't change the past, at least I can maximize the effect of the positive experiences and learn from the mistakes.

So far as the future is concerned, I approach it with positive expectations and ordinary caution. I'm not obsessed with its importance, nor do I rely on it for satisfaction, nor do I approach it with trepidation. Don't get me wrong, I'm all for the future, but what really excites me, turns me on, and gives me goose bumps is the present. It's the day I've got, the one I'm sure of, and I make the most of it.

2. Work is a blessing to be enjoyed. It's important to believe that one of the "blessings of life" should be your career. Too many people expect little more out of their toil than the paycheck they get at the end of the week and some sort of security package. That's just not enough for me. We spend more of our waking hours at work than anywhere else, and it's a pity to demean that precious time. How can we believe that we deserve to enjoy our life, and exclude the third of it devoted to making a living? Our work has to be more than an unfortunate necessity, an unpleasant means to paying the bills. We owe it to ourselves and the people who are important to us to demand more out of all those hours. It's our responsibility to make sure our work gives us the pleasure of pride, accomplishment, and congenial relationships. If the work we do fails to provide this joy, important changes should be made.

You may wish you could turn back the clock to the time when you embarked on your present career, and go off in a different direction. Even though it's not unusual for people to change fields, it does get more difficult the older you get and the more responsibilities you have. Frequently, people discover that they're just as frustrated and disappointed in the new field as they were before. It's really important to know the root cause of one's discomfort or disappointments. It might be the job, but not always. Very often it's the person.

A well-educated and personable young woman made an appointment with me to discuss a career change, hoping to connect with IBM.

"Mr. Rodgers," she said. "I've been in publishing for the past three years and I simply have to get out. I feel stifled, cramped. I can't tell you how drab and limited this field is. I've been an editorial assistant since I started; that's a glorified title for a secretarial gofer." She ran on nonstop. "People have the idea that publishing is one of *the* glamour industries. Well, let me tell you that's a myth; so is the notion that it's a beehive of creative activity. I have absolutely no opportunity to be creative or use my education and skills."

"Have you tried any other publishers?" I asked. "The directory's full of them."

"This is my third company. I never got fired; I survived two reorganizations, and it was always my decision to leave.

Publishers are all the same. Maybe ten percent of your time is spent dealing with publishing issues and ninety percent tangling with their bureaucracy."

I interrupted at that point. I'd heard this lament many times and I kept coming back to the same conclusion:

Businesses aren't boring—not the publishing business, not the shoe business, not the computer business. People are boring. Drab, unexcited, unmotivated people carry their boredom with them. They take it from job to job, hoping that they'll be brought out of their doldrums by a new job, new people, and a new environment. It rarely works that way; unfortunately, they usually bring down the new people around them instead of being elevated by them.

I suggested that before she started looking for a new field to go into, she examine her attitudes and her motivation. I told her I couldn't think of any business or profession that can't be intellectually stimulating; but exciting employees have to provide that stimulation. This young woman wasn't thinking in terms of being stimulating; she was looking for an employer to stimulate her. You may think I'm taking one side of the chicken-egg argument, and perhaps I am, but each of us is responsible for bringing excitement and energy to the workplace. It won't be in your job description, but you should behave as though it is.

If you feel bored, penned in, unstimulated, and unmotivated, it's your responsibility to do something about it even if the company you work for seems apathetic about the conditions you perceive to be the cause.

The young woman didn't need to change fields; not at that point. She needed to change her attitude and perform at a level that would bring her the fulfillment and pleasure she hoped for.

I suggested she stay on the job for six more months and not

only concentrate on doing outstanding work but really try to charge the environment with her own excitement.

"Call me," I said, "once you've driven the boredom out of your job. Then, we will talk about a career change."

She did call, about three months later, but not to talk about a career in information processing. She had begun to carve an exciting niche for herself in publishing. She was being promoted and her life was more satisfying. She had merely needed an attitude adjustment.

A business or professional environment is in many ways analogous to the city or town you live in. Your happiness isn't determined by how much a community has to offer you, although that's certainly a factor. The really important elements include what you do with what's available, how much of yourself you're willing to give to the community, and whether or not you enjoy the people you meet.

Indeed, it's great to work in an environment you really enjoy, but in time you will begin to enjoy any environment you're successful in.

We were created to enjoy life, including that part of our lives we devote to our work; but we must realize that all happiness is our responsibility. We're certain to be disappointed if we expect it to come as a gift.

3. We mustn't handicap ourselves with unrealistic expectations. One of the surest ways to experience frustration and unhappiness in your career is to carry with you a set of expectations and aspirations that are not rooted in reality. I don't know who suffer more, people who underestimate their own abilities and potential or those who overestimate them. But many people in both groups run into a lot of unnecessary disappointments because they build too many of their dreams on misunderstandings, inadequate information, and vague promises.

Why do so many people face each workday with so little joy or enthusiasm? Commuter trains, freeways, subways, and buses are packed every morning with people who wish they were headed somewhere other than their jobs. Things didn't work out for them—not the way they expected. It's sad, but it's not surprising.

Aside from those whose professions require long-term planning (doctors, lawyers, scientists, etc.), the majority of white-collar workers drift into their careers. We graduate from school or college and "get a job." It takes a while and generally several jobs for most of us to settle into a field. Sometimes the experimenting stops because we land in a business or an industry that feels comfortable and promising. The chemistry's right. As often as not, though, personal circumstances bring the experimenting to a screeching stop: maybe a marriage, a baby, or other financial obligations.

We leave an awful lot to luck, considering that next to our immediate families, the company we work for quickly becomes our most important and intimate relationship. As with most relationships, success at the job depends on what kind of mutual expectations we have and how realistic those expectations are.

Most of us approach employment the way we approach a blind date—with enthusiasm, high hopes, and very little information. We're perfectly willing to go through an almost totally one-sided screening procedure designed by the company. We present our carefully worded résumés, submit to a battery of tests, and are on our best behavior during the interview. If you're like most job candidates, you are so relieved, pleased, and flattered to be offered the job that you didn't bother to find out much more than the starting salary and whatever information the company volunteered. *So in the beginning, at least, the company protects its interests more than we protect ours.* It starts off with a more realistic expectation of the relationship than we have. It's no wonder that so many people are unpleasantly surprised once they get inside a company.

The possibilities for an initial disappointment are numerous. A new employee may believe the entry level position he accepted will prepare him for more responsibility and status. He soon discovers it's been a dead-end position for his predecessors and likely to be the same for him. He's expected to plug away at the job or leave!

New salespeople are often on the wrong end of a surprise if they don't learn what the average commission is and how much the most productive salesperson earns. If they accept a position without asking about escalating quotas, the frequencies of relocations, and how often territories are cut, the surprises could be devastating.

How many people suffer career disappointments because they didn't find out up front that the only ones in the company who earned more than a minimum living were the principals or that most important positions were filled by raiding a competitor's staff; or that little of the company's profit was reinvested for expansion or earmarked for continuing training and education. No matter how much homework they did in advance, they didn't find out enough about the company, nor did it find out enough about them.

To know what to expect realistically from a company, you should know something about the following:

- The company's beliefs, values, and culture.

  Some companies are put together to turn quick profits, with no long-range plans. To some, the customer is a one-time mark to be taken advantage of and dropped. There are companies that even today discriminate against minorities and women. Some are extremely paternalistic and protective. Others may display little or no interest in the employee, their only concern being his performance. Some strive to develop a family atmosphere and make certain social demands on the employee. There are businesses that depend on a continual turnover of its employees (direct-sales organizations, for example), and those that depend on developing long-term relationships with employees. If your beliefs and the company's are miles apart, you know that you're in for trouble.

- Its style, policies, terms, and conditions.

  Does the company have a competitive spirit? Does it encourage debate? Have a merit pay system? Put a high value on continuing education? Tolerate the wild ducks and royal dissenters?

- The quality of the people.

  There's nothing snobbish about this, but you can tell a lot about a company by the company it keeps. If you discover that it loses its most productive people, that those you meet are sour, cynical, and openly critical of the organization, you will be setting yourself up for a fall if you expect too much.

- Its products and services.

  If you're an engineer, a designer, or a production person who thrives on quality projects, your expectations can be shattered if you join a company that focuses on cutting corners. If you're a salesperson who likes to make quick sales by selling price and discounting, your expectations are going to take a bump if you find yourself in a company that stresses customer service.

- Its concern about you.

     Anyone who has hopes and expectations of building a lifetime career with a company must look at the record. Does the company have a full-employment practice? Does it promote from within? Does it invest in the continuing training and education of its employees? If you are a woman or a member of a minority group, has the company demonstrated fairness and sensitivity, to your satisfaction?

- Your growth potential.

     You can make money in any field you're in. Every industry has its share of spectacular successes; but average earnings are not equal in all businesses or professions. If you're in a field that has a lower than average earnings potential and you have big-money dreams, you're certain to bruise your expectations. If you want an annual six-figure salary with a liberal expense account and a good profit-sharing package, don't plan on spending twenty-five years as a straight-salaried salesperson in a family-owned business—not if it's somebody else's family.

4. Use all your talents. Don't overlook them. Make the most of them. If we recognize and express our many qualities, we can create a world of satisfaction and joy for ourselves. If we know ourselves well enough to draw out and exploit our capabilities, we'll never waste time envying others. We only need the wisdom to appreciate what we have and the resolve to make the most of our talents and virtues.

Too many of us sell ourselves short. *The problem most suffer is not shooting high enough.* So many people I've worked with downplay their talents, strengths, and attributes and eat themselves up worrying about their weaknesses. What a waste of energy! I say *go with your strengths, build on them, and work your talents as though they were muscles that will turn soft and useless unless they're exercised. Recognize your weaknesses without dwelling on them.*

5. You must believe in yourself. Know that you can take charge of your life. Successful people usually give themselves a fair share of the credit for their accomplishments. People who fail blame it on bad luck, fate, or enemies. They don't think that they contribute to their own misfortunes; nor do they believe they can effect a change. I meet too many people who seem to be drifting aimlessly or are in limbo. Ask them what they're waiting for, why they don't get off their backsides and start moving. They'll tell you they are waiting for the right time, a stroke of good luck, a rescuer. Hearing them talk, you'd imagine them as a vehicle with no steering device, with no control over what happens to them.

There are people whom I've admired for their kindness, warmth, and caring, people who are truly concerned about others. They seem willing to do almost anything within their power to help someone else, but won't give themselves a break. When they talk about themselves, the message is, "I have nothing to offer, nothing to contribute, nothing that makes me worthwhile or special." They look at successful people with awe, not understanding that what separates them from many of the people they envy may be little more than their own lack of self-appreciation.

To be successful, you have to believe you can change the conditions in your life. You have to get out of the back seat of someone else's car and get behind your own steering wheel. You can't wish away the things in your life that make you unhappy and you can't daydream your hopes into reality. You have to consider options, reach decisions, take steps, make moves. Make things happen.

6. Believe that you make a difference. The people I enjoy working with most are those who believe that we all can have an impact on the world around us. They're determined to use their power to effect the most positive changes possible. The people who sadden me most are those who don't believe they can make a difference. They become part of the so-called silent majority, hoping that someone else will take action against those things that need changing. What is needed is the vocal many—people of action.

I expressed these thoughts to a casual friend who seemed to be the kind of person who'd "give you the shirt off his back." So I was surprised by his reaction.

"Some of us manage to slip through the day virtually unnoticed." He smiled sadly and then continued: "And I'm one of them, I think. I envy the movers and the changers—they have something to offer—but I don't know how you can say that anyone can make an important difference."

"I say it because it's true. Look, you're affecting me right now," I said. "I want to take you by the shoulders and shake the hopelessness out of you. The point is that, like it or not, you made a difference to me. You affected my thoughts this morning, my attitude and mood."

He began to apologize, and I saw that he was really uncomfortable, so I dropped the subject. A few minutes later, he had what could have developed into a noisy argument with our waiter but went out of his way to avoid it. He had ordered broiled scallops, and the waiter brought fried scallops. He pointed out the error, and the waiter became defensive and unpleasant, claiming that he took the order as it was given him. My friend quickly backed off.

"It's okay. Maybe I did say fried. It doesn't matter. This will be fine."

After the waiter left the table, I said, "He was wrong."

"I know; I never order anything fried."

"He was wrong no matter what you ordered."

"Yeh, it's a damned shame, isn't it, the kind of help they get in an expensive place like this. Someone should do something about it."

"You're right, someone should." Then I almost shouted at him: "What about you? You're someone!"

That's the point, isn't it? We're all somebody and we all can make our presence felt. My friend agreed that if he owned the restaurant, he'd want to know about such an incident. The waiter not only made the lunch less pleasant for us, he probably cost the owner a couple of customers.

"Make a statement," I coaxed him. "Make something happen."

On our way out of the restaurant, he did. He described the incident to the maître d', who insisted on removing the cost of the meal from the check, and assured us that he'd deal with the waiter as soon as we left.

7. Don't take yourself too seriously. The people who are most comfortable in their skins are those who see the humor in their lives, even when in the most uncomfortable situations. They're not embarrassed to talk about personal experiences in which they simply forget to do something or were criticized for an action taken. They know that the world will recover from their mistakes, and they don't expect perfection from themselves.

I'm not suggesting that everyone turn comic—but when we give ourselves permission to lighten up, our performances improve.

8. Believe that people are basically good. It's a terrible thing to be a cynic or to assume that everyone is motivated by selfish reasons. I cannot imagine going through life always suspecting the worst about people, believing that everyone wants to take advantage of me. That doesn't mean that I leave the ignition key in my unlocked car or carry my wallet in my hip pocket or buy real estate from someone who pressures me to close an hour after I met him. I'm not foolish, either. I've made a few mistakes by letting someone into my life who really did want to use me; but I've made some wonderful friends, because I was open and honest and assumed from the start that they were good people. It's important to enjoy people, especially those you have to work beside or do business with. There are those who believe that people are basically bad and somehow climb over enough backs to attain positions of power and importance; but their paranoia and cynicism prevent them from enjoying success. Most cynics don't get very far, though. The walls they build around themselves to keep other people from getting in prevent themselves from getting out. Keep in mind—expect good from people and you'll probably get it.

9. You must pay your civic dues. When Tarshish talked about using your talents, he said: "You shall use whatever gifts God has given you, not only for yourself but for humanity." Nothing can nurture one's self-esteem more quickly than sharing one's gifts or talents with others. Not only is it important to become involved with people outside your home or business when you're struggling to establish yourself, but it's imperative once you've "arrived."

It doesn't matter what you do to give something back to the community in which you live or work, only that you do something. There are so many good causes: programs that combat drug and alcohol abuse; equal rights for the handicapped, minorities, women, gays, the elderly, the poor; mental health. There are civic groups devoted to beautifying the community and others that work toward making it safe.

Throughout my own career, I made what I call "paying my civic dues" a matter of personal and business policy. I structured it into my life. Years ago, I decided to give as much of my free time as possible to students on college and university campuses, and when I was in a strong enough position, I influenced the leadership of IBM to do the same. Today, IBM has an active program that covers hundreds of campuses. It's one of the most effective programs in America today that brings business and academia together, each raising the consciousness and understanding of the other. Although I've retired from IBM, I still visit and lecture at eight campuses a year. It's my way of giving something back to the institution that did so much for me.

So if you aren't satisfied with the way your career is developing, and really want to do something about it, I suggest you start by committing yourself to these beliefs:

- Life is to be enjoyed.
- Work is a blessing.
- Be realistic in your expectations.
- Develop your talents and abilities.
- Believe in yourself.
- Every person can make a difference in this world.

- Don't take yourself too seriously.
- People are basically good.
- We all have a civic rent to pay.

It all adds up to one's quest for self-worth and self-respect, without which there can be no real success.

3

Respect: The Company's Responsibility

I believe that it's the company's responsibility to put in place policies and practices that will nurture the respect of its people and be intolerant of their disrespect. Some things take very little effort and no expense; for example, treating people courteously. It may seem incredible to some of you that common courtesy is being discussed in a book written for adults; but it has to be discussed because this is a book about motivation, performance, and productivity, and shortfalls in all three are often caused by the insensitive way people behave toward one another.

A business must do everything it can to develop a work environment where people are respected. Many companies invest in the image or personality they want to project to their customers through advertising campaigns and the choice of their media spokespeople. They don't, however, pay enough attention to their real personality, which is a manifestation of their culture. That personality—not one invented by creative writers and professional actors—affects the company's internal performance and productivity level.

You don't have to spend many minutes in a place of business to characterize its personality. Is it friendly, nervous, scared, or a bully? Is it unorganized, compulsive, or disciplined? Is it healthy or sick?

Often the work environment in a company is a reflection of the personalities, attitudes, and behavior of its top management. What they think about their employees and how they treat them have a powerful impact on how the employees treat one another.

Does top management consider employees to be an important resource, an investment worthy of sensitive care and maintenance? Or does it think of its employees as an expense, a head count, something to be reduced whenever possible? It makes a big difference in the work environment.

IBM, one of the most respected companies in America, according to *Fortune* magazine, has never laid anyone off to reduce costs or for any other reason. The company's employees are its greatest resource and they know it. The fact that the company acknowledges their importance and demonstrates it in dozens of ways gives them pride, self-assurance, and a feeling of partnership with top management, the board, and the stockholders. They don't feel like an expendable, necessary-for-the-moment expense item.

There are lots of ways a company can show respect for its people and help them build self-respect and self-confidence. Some methods take time, planning, and investment—things like recruiting and hiring procedures, training programs, continuing education, and incentive packages. We'll talk about those later, but many of the most important ways take no more than a little thoughtfulness and commitment. To do the most good, these things should emanate from top management. It won't take long for the changes to echo throughout the company.

ACKNOWLEDGE THE EXISTENCE
OF OTHERS

When a person who's risen to the top echelon of a company averts his eyes when he passes a fellow employee in the hallway, or when he seems totally unaware that there are other people in the elevator, he's sending out an ugly message: "You are not important enough to acknowledge." I don't think that's the message most of such offenders intend to broadcast. Some top executives I know are shy, and at times awkward when they're thrown into a casual business situation with people they have little contact with. Some executives have such a difficult time remembering names they're afraid of making a mistake or telegraphing their problem; and some, of course, are preoccupied to the point of self-hypnosis. They truly aren't conscious of the people around them. They feel invisible.

A young department head was considered rude and something of a self-centered snob by many of the people he worked with and by those in adjacent departments. He was friendly enough conducting business in his office, but he rarely acknowledged their presence in the halls, the elevators, or the rest room. One day, his wife, who had just returned from a trip out of town, dropped in to surprise him. He was away from his desk when she arrived, and she stood in the hall outside his office chatting with his secretary, when she spotted him charging down the hall. He whizzed by the two of them, sideswiping his wife when he took a sharp right turn into his office, and he didn't say a word. The secretary, who was constantly being hurt by his slights, realized that at least some of his rudeness was caused by his intense concentration.

I don't think there are any acceptable excuses for not acknowledging another person. Every one of us should greet the people we pass in the halls or share an elevator with. If we know their names, we should speak them! We all know that nothing makes a person feel more secure than being addressed by name by a friendly voice. It's a gift we can give throughout the day, if we'd just think about it. To a stranger, passed in the hall, a warm salutation says, "Greetings, I work here and I'm proud of it."

Respect for others is the bedrock of all relationships, even the most casual, and must be demonstrated whenever we have the opportunity. In a business situation, it's an imperative.

If you avoid acknowledging people because of your position or status or because you don't need them, then shame on you. However, if your behavior can be interpreted as rude, insensitive, or uncaring, though you're merely shy, forgetful, or preoccupied, you must develop the skills to overcome these deficiencies.

There's another form of not acknowledging the existence of another person, which really bothers me. Here are two typical examples:

I had lunch with an officer of a large company. I met her in the lobby of her company's building, and on the way to the exit, we stopped before a group of three people. She introduced me to two of them: the head of an important research project and the company's comptroller. As we chatted for a moment or two, the third member of their group—the one I hadn't been introduced to—took a couple of backward steps and a half turn and deftly separated herself from us. She had been made to feel uncomfortable, unimportant. I kicked myself mentally for not having introduced myself to her; but before my companion and I headed for the door, I walked over to the young woman and shook her hand, and we exchanged names.

At lunch, I asked about her. "Is Mary with your company?" Frankly, I hoped that my lunch companion didn't know her.

"She works for Lou [the comptroller]. One of the secretaries in his office."

Apparently, she didn't think the secretary was important enough to be included in the introductions. Worse, neither did Mary's boss.

This was a blatant act of disrespect and to me, an outsider, it reflected negatively on the whole company.

As an associate and I prepared for a meeting one day, he referred to a participant as a nebbish. I knew the Yiddish word was a put-down, but I didn't know exactly what it meant and asked for a definition.

"They're the kind of people who sort of fade into the background." Then he added, "In a crowd, the nebbish is the one you always forget to introduce to your friends."

". . . because they're not important enough to be introduced to them," I tacked on. "Right?"

"You got it! You see 'em every day," he said.

"No, I don't."

"That's because they're invisible." He laughed.

"No! No one's *that* unimportant. If nebbishes do exist, they were created by self-centered boors who enjoy convincing vulnerable people that they have little value."

"C'mon, Buck, you're making too much of this. It's only a word."

Insensitive behavior repeated often enough by enough people in a company becomes an ingrained part of that company's culture. It becomes, in part, a snubbing system and absolutely has a negative impact on the performance of people it victimizes. *The leadership of a company must do everything possible to give credibility to every employee and to discredit any actions that even remotely encourage a caste system within their organization.* I don't like the idea of reserved parking spaces, executive dining rooms, or unnecessarily large

49

offices for top management when everyone else is working in cramped quarters.

TEACH GOOD MANNERS

Every day, we are bombarded with discourteous and unkind behavior. Bad manners have no place anywhere and especially not in business. The things we tell our kids about saying "Please," "Thank you," and "You're welcome" should be reemphasized to employees who either never learned those childhood lessons or forgot them. Although too many companies tolerate what I consider people abuse, most of them at least understand the importance of being courteous to their customers. I don't think many companies have any idea what they lose in terms of efficiency and productivity because of the discourteous, unthoughtful way employees treat one another.

Bad manners and bad management usually go hand in hand. I have great difficulty with managers or supervisors who blow up at an employee's mistake, especially in front of other people. Certainly, errors should be pointed out and necessary steps taken to eliminate as many as possible. That may mean a serious talk if the quality of the person's work is dropping and the errors are becoming chronic. It may mean more training or closer supervision for a while. It may also mean transferring the person to a job he can better handle, or if the situation warrants it, firing him.

Bosses who blow gaskets and verbally abuse their employees aren't skilled managers. They often mistreat a person in hope of forcing a resignation. If the employee doesn't resign, this type of manager probably won't fire him. He hasn't the guts.

There are times when an employee should be fired, but there are no times when he should be kept on the job and humiliated. Few things bother me more than seeing a person being chewed out by his supervisor. No one is paid enough to be publicly berated and demeaned.

A company that's worried about its efficiency and level of productivity had better take a hard look at its management team. They may have product knowledge and technical skills, but what they can cost a company by deflating the ego of its staff and enervating its motivation may be no trade-off.

A company has a right to insist that individuals put aside personal differences in order to get the job done properly. Unresolved spats can evolve into enormous problems.

Here's a silly but costly situation that's taking place in a well-respected company I recently visited: Two people in a five-person department haven't spoken to each other in more than a year—and one is the manager of the department! What's even wackier is the fact that the manager didn't freeze out his assistant. It was the other way around. I'm not talking about two schoolkids who are "mad at each other." These are adults with responsible positions, working in a corporation that employs more than two thousand people. They communicate by passing terse notes, almost always delivering the messages when the recipient is away from his or her desk. The situation is common knowledge in their division and certainly demeans the manager's position.

It sounds like the plot for a TV sitcom and it might be funny if it weren't so pitiful—and costly. Because of the tension between the two, an unpleasant cloud hangs over everyone in the department. Work is carried out without zest or efficiency and certainly without fun. Rather than confront his assistant, the manager comes in early every morning to complete work that should have been done by her. Why doesn't he fire her? For the same reason he hasn't been fired for being an ineffective manager. The company, which obviously accepts inappropriate behavior, has never spoken to either of these people.

Although it may talk about excellence in the boardroom, the company nurtures mediocrity on a day-to-day basis.

Neither of the people in the story above admits to knowing why or how their feud started; but I was told by another person in the department that it began when the manager told an ethnic joke that deeply offended the other person. Instead of dealing with the offense directly and resolving it, the assistant let her anger creep into almost every facet of her performance. The company suffered most, as the other members of the department have to work harder to compensate for this childish behavior.

END ACTS OF DISRESPECT

So much of the disrespect that lowers a company's efficiency, reduces its profits, and tarnishes its image can be quickly corrected by a determined leadership. Though not directed at anyone specifically, these acts chip away at the company's self-esteem. Left unattended, they become a distasteful part of the company's personality. Here are a few preventives.

1. Insist that people come to work on time and work the hours they're paid for. Companies spend hundreds, even thousands, of man-hours negotiating salary increases with their employees—often debating for months over two or three percent—then individuals are allowed to increase their own pay rate without authorization by reducing the number of hours they work.

A supervisor told me of an employee who complained about the size of her last annual raise.

"I think a four percent increase is insulting," the employee told her.

"What do you think you deserve?" the supervisor asked.

"At least eight percent."

"Then the four percent raise I recommended is too high." The supervisor quickly explained: "You're paid to work from nine-thirty to five, with a half hour off for lunch. You chose the hours, but you're rarely at your desk before nine forty-five, and you take at least forty-five minutes for lunch. That half hour computes to seven percent of the day; add that to the time you spend making personal phone calls and visiting with friends and the fact that you're out of the building by five. I guarantee that you take what amounts to a ten or twelve percent raise on your own!"

Of course, the supervisor was correct; but since she was aware of the situation, she should have put a stop to it right away. I know that it's not an easy thing to do when it's a condition that's prevalent throughout the company.

I recently had a 9:15 A.M. appointment at a business that occupied twenty-five floors of an uptown Manhattan sky-scraper. A young man met me at the tenth-floor elevator at exactly the appointed time and led me down a long corridor past a dozen empty offices. In most of them, the lights hadn't been turned on, and several phones were ringing—unanswered, of course. My guide seemed annoyed or embarrassed, maybe both.

"We're on flexible hours, but most people are supposed to be here at nine. The place will begin filling up in the next ten or fifteen minutes, half of 'em carrying their brown bags— bagel and coffee."

"How does that make you feel?"

"Like a fool. The company doesn't seem to give a damn, but my boss happens to be an early bird and a stickler. I don't get any extra for coming in on time, and they don't get docked for coming in late. It seems unfair."

He's right; it is unfair. More than that, though, it's ridiculous for a company to put up with such sloppiness.

My immediate impression of the firm was that it's mediocre at best. What about the people who were on the other end
of those unanswered phones? What was their impression?
What about the work that wasn't processed that first half hour
or so each morning? If the company was getting everything
out in good order, it was either overstaffed or open longer than
necessary.

It doesn't require any special motivational skills to correct
this situation. When top management asserts that salary will
not be paid for time not worked, the situation will improve
dramatically. It's not abusive, disrespectful, or demeaning
when a company will not disburse full-time pay for part-time
work. In fact, allowing people to become lax in their work
habits is a sign of uninterest on management's part. To me,
that's being disrespectful.

2. Insist that phones are covered and phone calls returned.
The telephone, important as it is, can be a source of serious
frustration when it's misused. Improved use of this instrument
can certainly enhance the efficiency, productivity, and image
of any company—and I'm not referring to the important ad-
vances that have been made in the field of telemarketing. I'm
talking about answering the phone when it rings, taking a
message accurately, and returning a call promptly if it can't be
taken immediately.

Today more than ever, when almost every desk is furnished with a phone and many have direct lines, the person
who leaves his phone unattended is doing his company a great
disservice. It's bad enough to call a place of business and be put
on hold before you have a chance to ask for the party you're
trying to reach. It's deplorable to call a business place during
business hours and not connect with anyone.

Recently, I met with a business manager in her office. She

needed information from a department located in another part of the building. She dialed the number four or five times over a ten- or fifteen-minute period before anyone answered. When someone finally picked up the phone, she was told that the person she needed was busy, but would get back to her within the next five minutes. When the call wasn't returned within the promised time, she phoned again. Now the person she was trying to reach was away from his desk, but would return the call "as soon as possible." The business manager slammed down the phone, then sent her secretary to find the person and the necessary information. When I left for the airport twenty minutes later, the call had not been returned, nor had the secretary come back. The woman, frustrated and embarrassed, promised to forward the information to me, which she did. What happened was inexcusable and costly in terms of wasted time plus the damage it did to the manager's pride and my opinion of the company.

My office phone is answered promptly, as is every phone in any efficiently run company. If I'm away from my office—out of the building, out of the city, or out of the country—the caller is told when I will return the call. If I find out that I'm going to be more than a few minutes late in returning the call, my secretary will phone the party and confirm the new time. It's my way of showing respect for the person who wants to speak to me. It's also one way of showing respect to the company that's paying my salary.

It really bugs me when I'm in someone's office who continually interrupts our meeting by taking phone calls. It's rude, disrespectful, or a power play. I don't put up with it. I ask for the meeting to be rescheduled and leave.

No department or office should empty out during the lunch hour, at coffee breaks, or when there are departmental meetings. Somebody has to be there covering phones. It's as important as keeping the doors of the business open.

3. Insist that letters and memos be promptly answered. Just as it's not unfair or oppressive for a company to insist that its employees begin work on time and handle the phones properly, there's nothing wrong with insisting that mail be attended to promptly.

Too many employees have a proprietary attitude about the mail addressed to them—as though it's personal mail, to be handled in whatever manner they choose. I don't feel that way, nor, do I want the people who work for me to feel that way. Company mail is not personal mail and should be handled as expeditiously as possible.

When I write a letter or memo, I expect a quick response, and when I receive mail, I assume that the senders expect the same courtesy. Well, they get it whether they expect it or not. At IBM, my rule was that a letter from a customer had to be answered within twenty-four hours. If the letter was a complaint or detailed a problem, the reaction time was as close to immediate as possible: a phone call, a personal visit, a cable— whichever response seemed to be the most useful to the customer.

I treated the mail from my fellow employees with the same urgency I accorded that of our customers. When I asked for their input—whether of ideas, opinions, data, or information—I let them know when I needed a response, and they knew that I expected them to come through. In case of a delay, they were to let me know as quickly as possible. In turn, I responded immediately to their requests with the information —if I had it—or with the time and date they could expect it from me if I didn't. If I said, "You'll have it by Wednesday noon," they could bet on it.

When people within a company have to wait for days, sometimes weeks, for information, the business operation bogs down.

How many times a day do people say, "I'll get right back

to you," then don't. Their thoughtlessness always causes some embarrassment and irritation, but sometimes the consequences can be measured in dollars and cents—in orders that are canceled, in contracts that fall through, in prospects who "walk."

MANAGE YOUR MEETINGS

I know companies that institute all sorts of safeguards against employees' stealing time from them: time clocks, head counts, sign-ins, morning meetings that start the minute the workday begins, demerits for lateness—you name it. I don't like to see a company become paranoid about the time it buys, but I don't blame it for wanting to get its money's worth. What bewilders me is that many companies that try so hard not to be cheated by their employees cheat themselves by wasting the time they're paying for.

I don't know how much money is wasted each year by business on unproductive company meetings, but it runs into multimillions of dollars. Because the costs of most in-house meetings aren't expensed, the waste doesn't show up as a ledger item that can be easily examined and evaluated.

Many of the most wasteful meetings are those that are scheduled regularly. They are indelibly stamped into a company's agenda and convene out of habit—even though no one expects anything really useful to be accomplished. The "Wednesday Morning Review" might have been a good idea when it was dreamed up three years ago. Today, most participants agree—when asked—that it's useless, yet nobody bothers to cancel it.

Scheduled or impromptu meetings often take the place of a well-thought-out memo or a telephone conference call. I was especially conscious of such a waste at a meeting I was recently asked to "sit in on" as a consultant. It was scheduled to begin at ten o'clock and to be attended by eight department heads, six project managers (four of them would come from a company facility across town), and about a dozen assistants. At ten, no one was in the conference room except me and a person who was setting up a coffee urn and a tray of sweet rolls. At ten-fifteen, when the meeting finally convened, about half of the chairs at the conference table were filled, and four or five people were in the corner of the room, pouring coffee and selecting their Danish. The rest of the participants showed up within the next ten minutes and took their seats after a visit to the coffee and rolls. The truth is, it didn't really matter so far as the content of the meeting was concerned.

The division's vice-president opened the meeting by reading a memo that he said would be distributed that morning, and made a couple of announcements. Then he went around the table, asking each department head, "Anything new?" The meeting turned out to be a kind of laid-back, show-and-tell experience. Those who had something to brag about did. Those who didn't have anything to brag about passed. Most of the side comments were gratuitous and contributed little or nothing to the presentations. Shortly after noon, the division's business manager rattled off some year-to-date figures; then most everyone rushed out of the room to their lunch dates. I overheard two stragglers talking as they were gathering up their papers.

One, a tired-looking man who had doodled throughout the meeting, said, "Well, two down, three to go."

The other wagged his head. "I can't believe that before this day is over we'll have gone through five of these."

"We'd be more productive if we spent the day at the movies or jogging in the park."

"I think I'll skip lunch and take a swipe at my in box."

"Not me. It's impossible to think about accomplishing anything on days like this. Frankly, I think it's damned inconsiderate."

I agree. Management has to be more considerate of its people's time. Some of my most frustrating moments at IBM were routine committee meetings. The meetings, although scheduled to end at a specific time, were actually open-ended, and no matter how much time I reserved for them, they ran over. Usually, the meetings dragged on because of inconsequential small talk; but the inconvenience caused by the delay was not minor. It had the domino effect of messing up the calendars, not only of those required to attend those early-morning meetings, but of everyone we were scheduled to see the rest of the day. Of course, the inconvenience cascaded down the line.

There are times when the most expeditious way to get something done is to bring a group together around a conference table; but that procedure is overused and too often abused.

The meeting I first described was unnecessary. The proceedings were recorded by a secretary, who told me they'd be transcribed that afternoon and distributed the next morning to the people who had attended. She could have gotten each department head's statement by phone or note. Since there was no real interaction at the meeting, her compilation and distribution of their remarks would have done the job as effectively as the meeting—and in this case would have saved the company about sixty very expensive man-hours.

As important as the wasted dollars are, I think the real cost of such a meeting is the message it projects—lack of respect for the company's time and, of course, the individual's. Here are some of my pet complaints and their solutions:

1. Unnecessary regularly scheduled meetings. Every regularly scheduled meeting should be examined, price-tagged, and justified. Those that cost more than they're worth should be scaled down or dropped.

2. Overattended meetings. Regularly scheduled meetings have a tendency to grow in size. An effort should be made to keep the size of every meeting down. People who don't contribute should be excluded, and furnished minutes if they need to know what transpired. It can be difficult to cut people out of a meeting. Some feel it's prestigious to attend as many meetings as possible, regardless of their value. Secretaries and administrative assistants spend hours unnecessarily in meetings and then are paid overtime to get their routine work done.

3. Meetings that don't start or end on time. These are unfair and disrespectful to the people who take their calendars seriously. The meetings I conduct run on a precise schedule. They start at the announced time, and they adjourn at the announced time. Only people who are needed are invited, and anyone who's late knows that he'd better have a good explanation. No one makes a habit of being absent or late, because he's replaced before that happens. It's true that I'm a stickler for what I call "calendar integrity"; it's not idiosyncratic, it's a matter of respect: for myself, the people who work with me, and the company that pays me.

4. Meetings without agendas. It bothers me to go to a meeting where there's no real agenda—where the host hasn't asked anyone to prepare for it and isn't prepared himself. Usually, these are the routine meetings that proceed by rote, becoming a ritual that has no meaning except to pay homage to the schedule. Sometimes the open-ended, unstructured meeting is convened to bring a creative group together in hopes that after an hour or so of freewheeling, something useful will happen. It rarely does.

I attend plenty of terrific meetings where ideas dance all over the room, where everyone comes prepared not only to throw out his or her own thoughts but to respond to the ideas of others. The meetings follow an announced agenda and never run beyond the allotted time. The only people who are invited are those who are expected to actively participate and do. What makes these meetings special is the preparation, enthusiasm, and sense of urgency the leader brings to them, the careful selection of the participants, and the fact that everyone in the room knows there's no such thing as an idea that's too dumb or off the wall to be expressed.

5. The boss's impromptu meeting. Some people in management who spend long hours in the office often do not respect the time of those who put in a regular workday. For whatever reason, they come in early and stay until they accomplish what they want. Because of their open-ended schedule, they feel less pressure from the clock and have no qualms about pulling people away from their work to chat, lecture, or gossip. Sometimes this is necessary when a critical situation develops or for promotion announcements, but not when it's done too frequently or for no reason except to give the boss a break and an audience.

6. The inspirational quick fix. Companies frequently look to the outside for ways of motivating their people. They send selected employees off to meetings designed to heighten their "awareness," activate their creativity, and make them more sensitive. These affairs can last anywhere from a day to a week, and can cost a company tens of thousands of dollars in fees, wasted time, and salaries. I understand how this can happen. Top management senses that its company is showing symptoms of sleeping sickness and sends for a doctor—and there's always a new cure sweeping the country. Through the years we've had some beauties. Remember est? For a few hundred dollars per head, company decisionmakers learned, among other things, how to get in touch with their anger. They were screamed at, called scum, and forced to ask for permission to go to the bathroom. Companies sent their people off to sensitivity groups where they learned to touch and cry.

These things sound great at first, but unfortunately, they take on the dynamics of an isolated event—a three-day diet, a Monopoly tournament, a three-day wedding party. When it's over, it's over. There's no meaningful follow-up, even if such a thing is possible. The costly affair is usually good for a glowing report to the board, showing management's keen interest in enlightenment. At the same time I recognize there are some excellent outside programs like The Aspen Institute, The Brookings Institute, and the Menninger Clinic.

However, when it comes to meetings, I truly believe that less is a lot more: more efficient, more productive, more exciting. Use the time you save for more important things.

A company, like an individual, must be cognizant of its personality. It must be especially conscious of the subtle ways it influences the mood and behavior of its employees. It must not underestimate the importance of its leadership and role-model qualities as it affects the pride, self-worth, and productivity of its people.

4

"How Are You Doing?" "Depends on Who You Ask."

"**H**ey, how're you doing, Joe?"
"Me? Pretty damned good, I think. I mean, they don't put out comparative figures, but I gotta be one of the top producers in the department. It came up from the grapevine that there's a terrific position opening up; they have to be considering me. If they pass me up for one more promotion, I'm kissing them off."

"How's he doing?"
"Joe? He's a plodder. Works his butt off, but he'll never advance. Not ambitious. He's strictly a follower and likes it that way. That's good; everyone can't be a chief."

"Hey, how's Joe doing?"
"My husband? Better than most of our friends. He's never missed a paycheck since we married. We don't spend more

65

than we can afford, paid off our car last month, and spend two weeks at the beach every summer. He's doing okay!"

"How's your dad doing?"
"How do I know? He's never home! Goes to work before I get up, and comes home when it's my bedtime. He's got a pretty important job, I guess, but I wish he had more time to spend with me."

We each have to define success for ourselves. The criteria may be wealth and power, public recognition and approval, or maybe serenity and peace of mind. It doesn't matter if your goal is to become regional sales manager, CEO, or a terrific cook and homemaker. Your success will be measured against the goals you set for yourself and what others come to expect of you—whether you agree with their expectations or not.

"HOW'RE YOU DOING?"
"COMPARED TO WHAT?"

One reason for the mediocrity we lament is that so many people forget about their goals or treat them as though they comprised a company-imposed game to be played every year or so but weren't part of real life. These workers don't really know how they're doing, because somewhere along the road, they forfeited the game or at least stopped keeping score.

I think that people who stop setting new goals and looking

for new challenges and greater satisfaction are giving up on themselves. They are either suffering from a sad case of complacency or have lost their motivation.

They may have struggled to get to their present plateau. Then, at some point, they gave up reaching for the next level, whether in terms of title, rank, job satisfaction, or new challenges. Unfortunately, some of them never realize that it takes as much energy and cunning to hang on to what they've got as it does to improve the quality of their careers.

Many people who are dissatisfied with the position they're in haven't a serious thought about doing anything concrete about it. They accept their condition as though they're victims of circumstances beyond their control. They're stuck. They often wish away their lives, dreaming of retirement, praying that they can keep a job from which they derive little satisfaction until they're fully vested in their company's pension program.

I've known people who join a company with so much enthusiasm that they can hardly contain themselves. They seem like certain winners, but gradually they wind down. They change, and if you see them only occasionally, the difference is dramatic and obvious. The bright aura of excitement that made them sparkle has been replaced by a weak glow of indifference. You can see the change in their posture and hear it in their voice. Vitality and passion are missing from the cases they present and the arguments they make. They know something went wrong, but often avoid digging for the reasons.

Too many people feel underpaid, unappreciated, even mistreated, and hang on to their jobs as though there were no other options. They're like the resigned spouse who's too weak or frightened to take a stand, too tired or apathetic to change a bad marriage or break the relationship. What about such persons' self-esteem? What kind of figure do they present to

67

their friends and family at the end of the workday? If they're parents, what do they tell their kids about self-confidence, self-worth, and the relevance of their dreams about the future? What happens to them when they look in the mirror? No one deserves to be in this condition; if you think you are, you owe it to yourself to reverse the situation.

Even people with good jobs can lose their sparkle and contribute to the mediocrity of the companies they work for. They make decent money, have a certain amount of responsibility, and wield some power, but somewhere along the line, they consciously or unconsciously decided to slow down. They stopped taking risks and started playing it a little closer to the vest. They became more concerned about the inner politics of the company than its goals. They do their work almost by rote, discourage innovations, and ignore the stagnation that is surrounding them. Obviously, they hurt themselves—and not so obviously, their listlessness is contagious and often lowers the performance of their co-workers.

I've known good people who early in their careers got nailed to the wall for taking a strong independent position or arguing a cause that was unpopular with their superiors. Once burned, they lost their courage, said "to hell with it," and put their independence, along with their creative energy, in the closet.

There are lots of reasons why terrific people have the wind knocked out of them; and there are as many reasons why good people become victims of self-depreciation. It's imperative that, to avoid such a sad dilemma, you keep your career animated and vibrant. Pick and choose the battles you fight and don't make every problem a war. Don't become gun-shy when your challenges are thwarted. Go after those things you feel strongly about. That is certainly true if you expect your work to contribute happiness and fulfillment to your life. I don't mean that to build a satisfying career you have to climb the corporate ladder; some of the most successful people I know have no interest in moving "up," but strive to bring more quality and excellence to the position they have and intend to keep. They are revered, recognized, and rewarded for their achievements. For them, the quality of the job, not the position or title, is what matters. They are proud professionals. The point is that unless you're willing to examine your ambitions and dreams, evaluate their reasonableness, and develop a strategy to achieve them, you could quickly settle for a less satisfactory career than you should.

I'm a goal-oriented person. I like the feeling of movement and progress in my work and enjoy a challenge that requires action and commitment to achieve. I'm careful that the challenges I accept are realistic and the goals reachable. I'm willing to take risks, and I like to stretch for what I want; it's okay if the odds start off being unfavorable—they can be changed —but I don't waste my time reaching for goals that are unattainable.

Setting goals can be tricky, even treacherous. I know people who set goals so far out in the future that there's no way to develop practical strategies to achieve them. They become so farsighted that they stumble over everything underfoot. Because of their fixation with long-term goals, they don't take current assignments seriously enough. Consequently, they aren't successful at either end of the spectrum. They're not satisfying the current expectations others are putting on them, and they're not moving any closer to their professed goals.

In some cases, people who seem to sacrifice short-term successes for long-term dreams have unknowingly built failure into their "strategy." By demeaning or deemphasizing the importance of the here and now, they sidestep today's chal-

lenges and competition. They pretend that they've put themselves on hold, just waiting for the right time to make their
move toward the big prize that's way down the road, around
the bend, and over the mountain.

I worry about people who put themselves in a holding
pattern waiting for a magical moment that never comes. They
become dull, tired, and uninterested in what's going on around
them. They don't think in terms of achievable goals, so they
don't think in terms of success or failure. How are they doing?
Not well enough; they're just biding their time. Most successful
careers are accomplished by taking lots of little steps while
conscious of the long-range possibilities, paying close attention
to today's challenges and problems and those of the immediate
future.

It's great to have an ambition or a dream that you can
project two or three years out; but it's vital that you know what
you want to accomplish within the next few weeks. You must
have a sensible strategy and an implementable plan. You need
to build in checkpoints to help monitor your progress. It's a lot
easier to get to where you want to go if you have a reliable,
readable road map. The shorter the trip, the more precise and
detailed the map should be.

*Keep your ambitions and dreams alive and active. Evalu-
ate your goals regularly, monitor your progress, and be flexible
enough to take advantage of any changes that occur.* Your
keen and optimistic interest in your career is the best antidote
to complacency, apathy, and defeat—the key components of
what I consider businesses' sleeping sickness: mediocrity.

It's not easy to take a hard, long, honest, objective look at
our own performance or the factors that shape it: our attitudes,
the level of our motivation, and the quality of our work. If we
want to climb to the next plateau to make sure our job remains
meaningful, such an examination is the place to start.

HOW OBJECTIVE CAN YOU BE
ABOUT YOURSELF?

Most people do a better job of appraising themselves when they're successful than when they're not. In fact, those who consistently meet the goals or quotas set by or negotiated with management often become their own toughest critics. Why? Because the more satisfied management is with their perform-ance, the less pressure they get from their bosses, who in time, unfortunately, may take their top performance for granted. High achievers put the pressure on themselves so they won't relax, get smug, and begin to slip. They're the self-starters the help-wanted ads are forever begging for and they know they're good.

The further one is from being a top performer, the more subjective and less accurate one's personal appraisal becomes. That's true even if the goals were well-defined and understood and the game plan followed to the letter. *The person who consistently fails to meet his goals is certain to grade his per-formance higher than his boss will.* The difference between the two appraisals will often be the bonus points or handicap the person gives himself for extenuating circumstances. These may be the unexpected distractions that he believes prevent him from making the goals. Sometimes the distractions are acute—a sudden financial burden, illness, or family problem. Sometimes they are chronic drug or alcohol abuse problems or simply "not feeling up to par." Whatever they are, a person with real or perceived personal problems will probably give himself an "A" for just making it through the day without botching everything up.

Even if it's your nature to be a guilt carrier, you probably have no trouble rationalizing the level of your business per-

71

formance, no matter what the shortfall. Listen to your own explanations of why things don't pan out. "The buyer won't admit it, but he hasn't the authority to make a deal." Or, "He sabotaged my proposal; it was a power play." Or, "He's still ticked off at the rep who preceded me in the territory." We can get pretty creative. We rarely admit even to ourselves that we blew it because we weren't sharp, didn't do our homework, or got surly with a customer. I never read a salesperson's call report that blamed his own shortcomings for the loss of a customer, and I don't recall writing one, either.

"DON'T CALL ME AVERAGE!"

At a recent sales "rally" sponsored by the Columbus, Ohio, Chamber of Commerce and attended by more than two thousand salespeople, the lead speaker opened the affair by asking all the "average salespeople" in the audience to raise their hands. No one responded. He knew they wouldn't, but he had a point to make. "Some of you have to be average," he shouted. "It's the law!"

He paused long enough to draw a few laughs from the audience. Then he detached the microphone from its stand, walked to the edge of the stage, and roared into the mike, *"Are there any* superior *salespeople out there?"*

This time, hands shot up everywhere and the audience roared back its self-approval.

I'm sure this opening routine wasn't meant to be taken seriously. It was an effective icebreaker and set the tone for the motivational meeting, but what about that response? How many of the two thousand salespeople in that auditorium truly considered themselves above average? Probably all of them did. Granted, they reacted with some bravado and lots of good humor, but did they mean it? I'd bet on it!

There seems to be a paradox working, doesn't there? I'm saying that even the people who have given up on their future, those who have chosen the false tranquillity of mediocrity over the adventure of seeking excellence, consider their average performance to be better than average!

The truth is that when it comes to our own work performance, we rarely, if ever, give ourselves bad grades; not even a "C." We simply don't like to think of ourselves as just average.

I don't have a quarrel with an individual who overstates his value somewhat. It's to be expected, but it becomes a problem when over a period of time a person unilaterally lowers his goals and expectations, and grades himself on the depreciated criteria.

When a person with "C" capabilities does "B" work, he should be given an "A" for the achievement; but when a person who has demonstrated that he's capable of doing "A" work consistently turns in a "C" performance, he should be on very shaky ground.

It's not easy for anyone to do an accurate, objective evaluation of his or her own performance. The difficulty is compounded if you don't know what's *really* expected of you, and it's hopeless if you don't know what you want to accomplish.

In spite of the many problems of a subjective self-evaluation, there are clues that can help sharpen your insights and make the exercise useful.

I. You're probably performing okay:

- if you feel good physically and emotionally.
- if you are generally happy in your work.
- if you look forward to each day's challenge.
- if you enjoy and are comfortable with the people you work with and for.
- if you are proud of your efforts and contributions.

73

II. You're probably not contributing as much as you think you are:

- if you don't feel good physically or emotionally.
- if you're generally unhappy and agitated at work.
- if you hate to get up in the morning and go to work.
- if you feel that you're overqualified for your assignments.
- if you feel unappreciated and mistreated by your bosses.
- if you feel superior to peers.
- if you are suspicious and paranoid about the people under you.

If group I generally represents your feelings and attitudes, the company you work for is lucky to have you. You're probably fortunate to have landed a position with it, assuming that you're not living in a fool's paradise. If your perceptions are shared by the people you work for, your career's on track, and you have only to be careful not to be lulled into a state of self-satisfaction. You mustn't lose the excitement and edge that helped propel you to this pleasant position.

If you see yourself in group II, you may disagree with my assumption that you're probably overevaluating your performance. I suppose it's possible to feel lousy, hate your job, dislike the people you work with, and still turn in a superior performance. It's possible, I guess, if a person is overqualified to the point that he can do a better job by rote than others, less talented, must struggle to do. But unless such a dissatisfied person works pretty much in a vacuum, his negativism can "wash" his usefulness.

Whether or not you're overestimating your value to the company (if the feelings and attitudes in II accurately represent your own), your career is probably in trouble or rapidly heading for it. We'll get into the specifics later, but now we'll stick to the subject of how we think we're doing and how others might disagree.

III. You're probably not contributing as much as you should:

- if you feel beholden to or dependent on a "mentor" or "sponsor."
- if you'd rather bury yourself in the minutiae of your in-box than tackle the tough problems that should be high on your hit list of priorities.
- if you find yourself dropping your good ideas to avoid rejections.
- if you support positions you disagree with rather than face a confrontation.
- if you wish you had more training, better skills, or a deeper understanding of the world in which you work.
- if you feel pretty good about your work but not too happy about your relationships.

Although concerns about work may cross our minds, we seem to minimize their importance when it comes to evaluating our overall performances. No matter what, we manage to get a darn good grade—certainly better than average.

ABOUT THE COMPANY'S
APPRAISAL OF YOU

What about the management person who's responsible for evaluating your performance? Is his assessment much more objective than yours? Doesn't he bring to the examination his own biases, rationalizations, and personal problems? Of course he does, and it's unlikely that he'll factor into his appraisal the extenuating circumstances that raised the grade of your self-evaluation.

It's not easy to find out what your company really thinks about you. There's plenty of circumstantial evidence to draw from, but it's surprising how deftly the subject of one's performance is avoided. There are still plenty of firms that dole out raises and bonuses without any explanation or discussion of the factors that influenced the amount paid. If the employee complains, the supervisor tries to quell the discontent without hurting the complainer's feelings or escalating the conversation into a confrontation.

It's not unusual for a supervisor or manager to sidestep the issue of the employee's performance entirely and blame a disappointingly small salary increase on forces beyond either side's control—maybe a "budget squeeze," or a "downturn in profits," or "trouble with the gang upstairs," or "demands of the cost of living index."

If the employee accepts the explanation and lets the supervisor off the hook, both may breathe a sigh of relief. The supervisor avoids a tense situation, and the employee's intuitive evaluation of his own performance is untarnished!

Of course, everyone—including the company—is short-changed. The supervisor who obviously believes that the employee's work is not worthy of a better raise, or is reluctant to fight for one that is deserved, fails to use the opportunity to motivate that person to improve his performance. The employee comes away from the discussion thinking: The level of my performance has nothing to do with my salary increases, so I'll just coast along. The company's vitality suffers a blow and mediocrity scores another point.

Incredible as it may seem, there are people who work for companies for years and are never invited to sit down with their bosses to discuss the quality of their work or their career possibilities. This can happen when relationships get blurry, or when responsibilities and goals are poorly defined. I don't know which is worse, a misleading evaluation or none at all.

So how does one get a realistic fix on one's own performance? Many companies hope that a formal annual performance appraisal will do the job, and it has the potential for doing good. Its use is widespread among large companies and is growing throughout business and industry in general.

Originally, the annual appraisal was developed primarily to provide management with an orderly and evenhanded system for dividing annual salary increase and bonus pots. Some companies still use the procedure exclusively for that purpose, but other companies use it to open communications between employees and their managers.

If a management is truly interested in an open dialogue with its people, and if the employees welcome constructive criticism and are willing to really examine their performance with their manager, the annual appraisal can be a very useful motivational tool.

Every employee should come away from a serious appraisal with a fairly realistic view of where he stands with his supervisor and the company. He should know what management perceives his strengths and weaknesses to be. He should have a pretty good idea of where he's rated among his peers and what he has to do in the future to improve his rating. There's a lot that can come out of these evaluations if both parties are open and honest. However, if approached by either party with anything less than forthright candor, the exercise falls flat, becomes benign at best and demotivating at worst.

There are a number of variations for these annual evaluations, but they fall within four basic formats: (1) Excluding employees' participation, the supervisor or manager grades his staff and recommends salary increases to the powers above

77

him. That's it. Sometimes the employee doesn't know a formal evaluation took place and finds out about the raise when it shows up in his paycheck. Such evaluations are the least useful to the individual and to the company. (2) A step in the right direction requires the manager to show the employee his review and have him sign off on it. A discussion may ensue, but isn't necessarily encouraged. (3) Then there's a system wherein the employee contributes to the appraisal by writing a memo that describes his accomplishments for the year. The manager incorporates the employee's views into his own evaluation as he sees fit and shares the final draft with him before sending it on.

(4) In a more complex procedure, the employee and the supervisor or manager independently fill out a prepared form that covers every imaginable factor that might affect the employee's performance: understanding of the job, technical skills, knowledge and education, ability to communicate, creativity, attitude, motivation, work habits, level of efficiency, productivity, and so forth. Then employee and supervisor sit down eyeball to eyeball, and go over each point made in the two appraisals. The manager praises and criticizes, and the employee accepts the praise and rebuts the criticism. They manage to produce a single document on which both can agree. Examples three and four are obviously the better way. When the process is completed, there is an improved understanding of one another, with the appraisee knowing exactly what he must do during the next twelve months to improve his or her situation.

The formal performance appraisal is a time-consuming procedure and often creates an uncomfortable situation for the manager and the employee. It can be a helpful motivational tool if used properly, as we'll see later; misused, it can be damaging, discouraging, and nonmotivational.

The annual evaluation is certainly no substitute for good management throughout the year. When open, honest communication is sustained between the employee and his manager, this annual procedure becomes a review or formalization of their ongoing dialogue, and doesn't turn up any surprises for either party. That is the ideal situation. Some companies recognize the need and the right of employees to know how their work is being judged. A formal evaluation is conducted semiannually or even quarterly to facilitate more dialogue between the various levels. Unfortunately, when the communications aren't open and honest on a daily basis, they don't improve during the appraisal procedure.

Here's what happens too often: The manager or supervisor hasn't been straightforward with the employee for twelve months. He has allowed what he considers inferior work or inappropriate behavior to slide by because he has no stomach for a confrontation. It's unlikely that the manager who can't stand up to the employee during the year will get much braver or more candid at the appraisal meeting. Consequently, the exercise becomes a costly waste of time. The employee does not get a fair evaluation, nor does he come away with a realistic understanding of how he's doing. He's cheated. The manager probably wanted to unleash a flood of criticism, but he didn't have the guts. Or else he slid over the review as quickly as possible, as though it and the employee weren't very important. The manager wanted the meeting to end without getting into anything controversial. The employee comes away from the session thinking: Hey, I'm doing okay!

The employee ends up confused and discouraged when he gets a minimum raise and is passed over for more responsibility or a promotion. The double messages he receives are unfair and he has to reach his own conclusions: "This guy is holding me back because I'm a threat to him," or, "He doesn't like me." The boss will manifest his frustration in all sorts of unpleasant ways. Instead of sharing his concerns with the employee, he complains to his colleagues and sometimes to the employee's co-workers. He exacerbates the situation when he shows his displeasure by pouting or acting crabby or, worst of all, by freezing the employee out of the department's inner circle.

This employee is being sandbagged! He has a right to know what his boss thinks of his performance. Because he's not criticized, he's being led to believe his work is at least acceptable and may be superior. On the other hand, the manager-employee relationship is strained and unpleasant because the boss has internalized all his frustrations and concerns. What surfaces comes across as spiteful behavior and unattractive personality quirks.

You do a person a favor, in the long run, by leveling with him. People have a right to be told the truth about their capabilities and potential.

Good managers aren't born, they're trained. Too many people with no training and minimal or no managing skills find themselves "in charge" because they were terrific technicians, wonderful salespeople, or hard-working, loyal employees. Most companies have no formal management training programs. One can only hope for the best when someone is promoted to a position that requires him to be an organizer, a supervisor, a critic, and a motivator. It's difficult for the people who work for such managers, and it's not easy for the managers, either. They're all victims of antiquated, inadequate management practices, which have to be revamped.

Far too many white-collar employees have a truly difficult time getting a thoughtful, honest, useful evaluation of their general performance. For most white-collar positions, it's difficult to quantify the productivity of an individual. More jobs today are accomplished by people working in teams, and when the work isn't directly connected to the production or sale of a product or service, evaluation becomes even more subjective and complicated: How you're perceived becomes as important as how you perform.

5

The Projection Perception Connection

Careers can be made or broken, promotions won or lost, simply on the basis of one person's perception of another. If you think that's too strong, you'll certainly agree that perception can be the deciding factor when two or more people of equal ability are being considered for a promotion. We all know people who were passed up for an important assignment, not because they didn't have the skills to do the job, but because the decisionmakers didn't think the person had "it," or thought someone else had more of "it." The person who was passed by didn't project sufficient confidence, courage, leadership qualities, or objectivity to give him or her the edge. On the other hand, some careers that soar like a rocket are propelled by style and charisma rather than ability. Too often, though, the personality and character messages we project distort the truth about ourselves to our disadvantage, even to the point of our losing a legitimate competitive edge.

The *Chicago Tribune,* covering a recent workshop on getting ahead, quoted the leader of the group, an Illinois Department of Insurance official, as saying: "There have been several studies showing that successful executives spend about half their time actually working and the other half achieving visibility on the job."

I've never seen anything to support that statement and I hope that the speaker meant it to be hyperbole. There's no doubt in my mind, though, that most successful people are quite conscious of how they're viewed and do what they can to be positively perceived.

WHAT DO YOU WANT THEM TO SEE WHEN THEY LOOK AT YOU?

Maybe you have a pretty good idea of how you're perceived by others, especially the people you work with and for. If the messages they send back to you indicate acceptance, respect, and even admiration, you're probably pleased with the way you're being viewed, and probably should be. But if you don't like the way you're being sized up—if you feel shortchanged, misunderstood, and unappreciated—you'd better do something about it. Once you understand why people see you the way they do, you can begin altering the image you project—if you don't like what you see.

I know that some people are repelled by the idea of "changing" in order to impress someone else. Remember the old Flip Wilson punch line, "What you see is what you get"? Lots of people react that way. They think: If they don't like me the way I am, *they* have a problem. I say, if that's your attitude, maybe *you* have a problem—and unless you're chairman of the board of your own company, it could stunt your career. The point is, many people do a bum job showcasing what they've "got"; the package they present often doesn't do justice to the product within.

There's nothing deceptive or hypocritical about consciously doing something positive to alter the image you project. It's smart. It can accelerate a stalled career, but more important, it can both heal and activate an ailing ego.

86

Since each of us arrived on this page with a different set of problems, I'll cover more problems than you have to deal with personally, but the space won't be wasted: you'll recognize many as headaches of your associates and friends, and you will find ways to help them.

DEALING WITH THE MOST IMPORTANT PERCEPTION OF ALL

This heading refers to one's self-perception. After all, what we think of ourselves certainly influences what others see in us.

Most successful people have a fairly healthy ego. They know they're okay and transmit that confidence by their appearance, demeanor, words, and actions; and they expect others to recognize and appreciate their strengths and abilities. They are usually good role models and always good subjects to study. But even some successful people have more than their share of self-doubts and have trouble appreciating themselves.

"We are often our own worst enemies" is a cliché because it's so true. Sometimes we hurt ourselves by examining ourselves too closely, overanalyzing, scrutinizing, and magnifying every imperfection and weakness and overlooking every good quality and strength. Sometimes we wreck ourselves by not looking inward, by ignoring our own needs and burying our feelings as though they didn't matter.

I remember a song that began:

> *You look into the mirror*
> *And you don't like what you see.*
> *If you don't respect yourself, sir,*
> *What can you expect of me?*

It's not a great song, but it can hit a nerve. Most people expect more respect from others than they give to themselves. To me, it's a puzzling psychological quirk that makes us hope, even expect, that others will see more positive things in us than we see in ourselves; and we're disappointed, even dismayed, when we discover they don't like us any better than we like ourselves.

If the package or image you're presenting to the public suggests that you're not sold on yourself, you might consider some redecorating. If too many doors seem to close on you and you feel frozen in place, you'd better make sure you're not the one who's pulling the rug out from under you.

Let's start with the surface stuff. What do you see when you get a quick glimpse of yourself in a window reflection? Coming upon your image unexpectedly can be startling. You're hurrying down Fifth Avenue or Main Street to an important meeting, when out of the side of your eye you catch your unposed candid reflection in a store window. Gulp! Is that you? Your stomach has pushed your jacket out of shape, distorting your silhouette; your hair still has that seventies look; and there's an intensity about you that would frighten children.

What you see is what *they* see, and that impression is factor number one in their perception of you.

IF YOU DON'T LIKE WHAT YOU SEE

If you don't like your physical appearance, don't slough it off as though it doesn't matter. It's probably important to you, and it should be. Luckily, it's the easiest part of you to change.

The things that bother you about your appearance are probably not the same ones that bother others. You might be self-conscious about the shape of your nose, the size of your ears, your height, the texture of your hair or the fact that it's receding. Frankly, I don't think any of these things are very important to other people; but if you're truly uncomfortable because of a correctable cosmetic defect, do something about it. Change the color or style of your hair, try a pair of "elevator" shoes, grow a beard or shave one off. Get a new suit, some good-looking shirts, and a few up-to-date ties. And above all, stay in shape. The better you feel about yourself, the more attractive your projected image will be. I wouldn't plunge into major plastic surgery without a lot of counseling; I'd make sure that such a drastic action would make a major difference in my self-appreciation. But minor changes? Go to it.

Understand that these changes are primarily for you, not for someone else. Don't *over*estimate the importance of your "good looks" to others. The advertising people would have us believe that success and beautiful features are Siamese twins. That's only true in the thirty- or sixty-second TV commercials that are zapped at us day and night. Actually, in the business world I know best, *any* distracting appearance can be a handicap; and too much beauty can be a terrible distraction. In most careers, ordinary lookers have an advantage over the dazzling Raquel Welch and Robert Redford look-alikes. So before you opt for a major overhaul, start with a tune-up. In fact, before you do anything, make sure you've covered the following matters.

THESE THINGS WILL MAKE YOU
FEEL BETTER

1. Good health. Good health is unquestionably the number one appearance enhancer. Nothing will do more for the image you project or the one your mirror sends to you. Like happiness, good health radiates a pleasurable impression. If nothing else, it brightens and animates your presence.

Use common sense when it comes to your physical well-being. You know the benefits of a well-balanced, nutritious diet; you know that you should exercise regularly, not just on weekends; you know that smoking is unhealthy and foolish; and that moderate use of alcohol doesn't mean two or three cocktails at lunch, after work, at dinner, and before retiring.

Don't settle for just feeling fair. If you're experiencing minor but chronic discomforts, see a doctor; don't assume they're an inescapable part of maturing. Certainly, take advantage of the physicals covered in your health insurance policy. Let a physician tell you what it will take to make you feel great (and I don't mean with a chemical high); and then strive to achieve that wonderful state of being.

What about overweight? Carrying too much weight is a health hazard; but it also conveys a lot of negative connotations when it comes to image and perception. That's especially true when someone is excessively overweight.

Generally speaking, an obese person is competing with a serious handicap. Excessive overweight sends out a few unfortunate messages, which may or may not be true. Things like: "I have an obsessive nature, so beware of me"; "I have an underlying problem that manifests itself now in overeating—who knows what it will do next"; "I'm an undisciplined person"; "I'm a bum risk for any company or any new relationship —I'm just a step away from a stroke"; or, "I don't think too much of myself and don't expect you to."

Of course, I know fat people who should be excluded from the judgments above; they're wonderful, happy, well-adjusted people. But we're not talking about reality; we are talking about perception. The truth doesn't ease the pain when overweight individuals are obviously put off by other people. It has to hurt.

One of the most satisfying experiences in the world is watching the changes that take place when an obese person goes on a healthy weight-loss program and the pounds start melting away. I've seen incredible improvement in the person's personality, behavior, and performance after a weight loss. Just as dramatic is the change in other people's reactions and perceptions.

2. Resolve the moderate-overweight dilemma. Moderate overweight is a chronic pain in the neck (and often a real pain in the back!). The weight of most people over thirty-five or forty goes up and down like a yo-yo. We feel great about ourselves when we're down and we project that good feeling; and we feel rotten about ourselves when our weight's up, and project that too.

Moderate overweight is probably more a psychological than a health hazard. The constant fight to maintain our "ideal" weight is not only aggravating and frustrating; it's rarely satisfying. When we're successful, we bore our friends and colleagues with the gory details of how we did it. We become as self-conscious about our shape as a starlet on the beach, pretend to prefer lemon juice to blue cheese on our salad, and are never hungry enough to finish off a meal with something sweet. But sooner or later, most of us start giving in to the good things on the menu and our weight inches up. Pretty soon we feel like dopes and failures and know that somewhere down the line we'll begin the cycle over again.

Unless a physician tells you that the extra weight you're carrying is dangerous to your health, your weight problem may be more one of self-perception than anything else. You think everyone is looking at your bulges and it makes you uncomfortable. Well, if your weight isn't a health problem, then hide the bulges and forget them. It's as simple as wearing clothes that fit.

I don't think camouflage is necessarily a cop-out. There are times when you simply can't face another dish of cottage

91

cheese or three hundred calories in a six-ounce glass; you're not ready to even consider the best approach—a new lifestyle that incorporates a regimen of exercise and proper nutrition. You'll do it later, right? That's okay, but in the meantime don't be one of those people who begin each day by cramming their size 42 bodies into the size 40 suits they bought the last time they went on a blitz diet. Tight clothes make you look twenty pounds heavier than you really are. The extra weight hikes trousers up over ankles and puts a painful-looking strain on your waistband and belt. Shirt collars (if they can be buttoned) seem to be strangling you, and it's obvious that jackets can't be buttoned.

Women, I think, are less guilty than men of putting off updating their wardrobe to fit their figures. If you're one of the millions of people who suffer from the fluctuating-waistline syndrome, invest in a second wardrobe. Consider it part of the cost of doing business—a nondeductible but important expense.

Personally, I don't have a weight problem, but I suppose I would if I gave it a chance. I watch the scale and when my weight begins to creep up, I cut calories until I'm where I want to be. That doesn't happen very often, because I run five miles every day. Exercising has always been an important part of my everyday activities. Besides exercising for its own sake, I play a lot of tennis and golf. I've passed my sixtieth birthday and weigh a little less than I did when I was in college.

3. How one dresses is just as important today as it was fifty years ago. I've never read any of the "dress for success" books, but I know there's a need for them. I'm pretty much a traditionalist when it comes to clothes, as are almost all the successful business people I know. Studies have shown that people who dressed in business suits (men and women) were treated with more courtesy, respect, and attention than those who conducted business in sports clothes or in other casual dress. They projected professionalism and efficiency. Remember, we're still talking about image and perception.

It became fashionable a few years ago to "thumb the nose" at traditional business clothes. They became a symbol of the Tired Old Establishment. Dress codes were looked upon as one method a dictatorial management used to squelch individuality and personal expression. I said "Baloney" then, and I still say it. It's distracting when people are "out of uniform." I don't want the nine millionaires who take the field for the New York Yankees to express their individuality by wearing whatever they choose. I don't want the maître d' at my favorite restaurant to greet me in a sweatshirt and a pair of walking shorts. I don't want my tennis partner to show up on the court in cut-off jeans; and I don't want my company's salespeople to call on customers dressed as if they're going to a company picnic. It's distracting, sends out the wrong messages, and reduces effectiveness.

If you want to change your image and get an immediate boost in self-appreciation, examine and update your wardrobe. Buy well-tailored business clothes to conduct your business in, and see the change in the way people react. Dressing appropriately for business doesn't mean losing your individuality or looking drab. For thirty years, I've worn a handkerchief in the pocket of my suit coat. It picks up the color or colors of the tie I'm wearing, but not the pattern. It may be an idiosyncrasy, but it's become my trademark. Some people do it with a tasteful piece of jewelry, a hat, a stylish bag, or an attaché case; and some make very subtle statements that they keep pretty much to themselves—maybe very expensive undergarments or flashy suspenders. I'm all for making a little statement that's not extreme or distracting, one that says, "Hi, world, *I'm me!*"

4. Good grooming and good hygiene are for adults too. I played with the idea of skipping this subject on the grounds that it's too obvious to deal with, but sometimes people forget about the basics. The difference between success and failure often depends on the way we attend to those things we might tend to take for granted. If anything can screw up the image you'd like to project, it's failing to pay attention to simple details.

You can leave your home in the morning looking great and smelling clean (or not smelling at all), but halfway through the workday be disheveled, rumpled, not so clean, and smelling not so sweet. Check yourself out during the day; it's just as important that you look fresh and clean for your three o'clock appointment as you do for the morning meeting.

5. First you're seen, then you're heard. What you sound like and what you think you sound like have a tremendous impact on the image you project and the impression you make on others, especially the first impression. The sound and tone of your voice, your diction, and your language skills can be terrific pluses for you, or they can be negatives and unnecessary burdens. *Unnecessary* because most offensive or distracting vocal communication habits can be easily corrected once the problem is recognized and a decision is made to do something about it.

Some people talk too loud. They can overwhelm, embarrass, or intimidate another person simply by the size of their voice. I know a very talented, hardworking sales rep who competed more than once for a management position and was shot down each time, because he was too loud. He's an embarrassment at any public gathering. His booming voice and laugh can draw everyone within earshot into his private conversations. Worse than that, he infringes on the privacy of a party halfway across the room. What's so frustrating about this particular case is that this man is very bright, strongly service oriented, and quite innovative. He has lots going for him that should qualify him for serious managerial consideration; but it won't happen until he can put a volume control on his voice box.

Rightly or wrongly, people with extremely loud voices are often perceived to be overly aggressive, exhibitionistic, or insensitive. They may be none of these things, but have handicapped themselves with this perception—one that could easily be corrected. Sometimes people talk very loudly because they don't hear well. Forget your vanity and start wearing a hearing aid. It's foolish to do otherwise.

Some people who talk softly can put others off as much as their loud counterparts. People with very small or extremely quiet voices don't embarrass me the way the boomers do; but they damage their image needlessly. This may be unfair, but I usually perceive these people as falling into one of three categories:

(a) The weaklings—those who lack self-confidence. They don't think what they say really matters to anyone but themselves and wish they were somewhere else. Their posture and demeanor usually support this perception. They seem turned inward, bunched together, and uncomfortable. I feel uncomfortable because of what I perceive to be their distress.

(b) The manipulators. I feel that the hushed tones of these people are contrived to put me at a disadvantage, that they're trying to force me to concentrate on every word they utter. They may sit on the edge of their chairs, their eyes locked on mine, droning in a quiet, intense monotone like a hypnotist trying to induce a trance.

(c) The snobs. These people give me the feeling that they don't care whether I hear them or not. They broadcast their wisdom on forty kilowatts, mumbling, grumbling, sometimes smiling at an inside joke, making me feel as if I were eavesdropping on a private conversation. I remember being at a meeting dominated by three of these types. They must have attended the same school of charm and elocution: They all slouched in their chairs, stroking the side of their nose, their chin, and their lips, with their eyes drooping to the point where I wasn't sure if they were awake or asleep. They were awake, of course, and all seemed to know what the others were saying, although I had a terrible time translating their mutterings. I was certain they must all be lip-readers. The first time I entered the discussion, my voice sounded like the blast of a trumpet. They didn't react, but it almost lifted me off my seat. It crossed my mind that I was the butt of a practical joke. I half expected Allen Funt to cry out, "Smile! You're on *Candid Camera!*" That meeting took place a long, long time ago. I wouldn't sit through one like it today.

THE COMPULSIVE TALKER

No one wants to be perceived as boring or scatterbrained, so why do so many people talk compulsively? Why, once they get the floor, do they seem determined never to relinquish it? Why do they run on without taking a breath, fearing that if they pause, someone else will start talking and they'll never get another chance? That's not the image they want to project, but that's how they impress me.

None of us want to give the impression that we're fast-talking wisecracking con men, but plenty of us do. None of us want to sound like whiny hypochondriacs, but plenty do. None of us want to come across as uncouth, dull, shrill, or hysterical. Many do, even though they don't want to and don't have to.

If you don't like the sound of your voice, your diction, or your delivery, do something about it. You can be trained to raise your voice, lower it, or give it more resonance. Actors, athletes, and many business people invest time and money to improve their voice. I encourage anyone who is uncomfortable speaking, even in front of a few people, to join a local Toastmasters Club or enroll in a Dale Carnegie course. As IBM's vice-president of marketing, I often sent people to the Communispond program. I understand that some people have found Dr. Morton Cooper's book *Change Your Voice, Change Your Life* useful. I'll talk more about these options when I discuss speaking before groups.

Think about how you want to be perceived, and then make sure that the way you look, sound, and behave contributes to that image.

6. Sound smart. Sometimes it's not the quality of your voice or even what you say that enhances or depreciates your image, it's your presentation. Years ago, I heard Benny Goodman, the great swing and jazz clarinetist, sing a song that included the lyrics: "It ain't what you say, it's the way that you say it—that's what gets results." The impact of *what* we say or do often depends on *how* we say or do it. Style is not all it takes to get results, but when it comes to perception, it helps. Like it or not, many people size us up by the language we use to communicate our thoughts and ideas. They evaluate our intelligence, our knowledge, our sincerity (or insincerity) by our choice of words. They think they know how well stocked our cranial library is by the way we verbalize. They may miss the mark by a mile, but perception is perception.

If you're embarrassed or insecure about your language skills and envy people who express themselves more fluently or succinctly than you, take a course in communication, creative writing, or even business-letter writing. Perhaps the most gratifying way to enrich your vocabulary, your imagery, and your confidence is to broaden your interests. Any new subject or interest will add color and texture to your communications.

Anyone who has gotten this far into my book knows that I'm not a linguist or a semanticist. I simply want to be understood. I want to project accurately not only my ideas and thoughts but also my intent; the level of my interest about the reader or listener and my enthusiasm. My ability to communicate is an important factor in my successful career. In dealing with many of the giants of business, industry, and academia, I have been able to make myself understood without using foreign phrases, obscenities, or a dazzling vocabulary. None of those come off my tongue comfortably or naturally.

There are people who use words like colors on an artist's palette, making use of an enormous vocabulary without sounding forced or contrived; but we all know folks who seem to be more interested in their verbal virtuosity than they are in the information they're trying to communicate. They may express themselves in esoteric terms, enjoying the feel of the words on their tongue and the sound of them in their ear; and they're not bothered if they end up firing semantic blanks at the people they're communicating with. Maybe they're trying to quickly establish the breadth and depth of their education, but in most cases, it is perceived as insensitive grandstanding. It's true that you can broadcast almost any kind of image you elect; but you'd better give some thoughtful consideration to the people you're trying to reach if you want their perception to jibe with the image you are projecting.

8. Be careful and make your changes cautiously. Some people are so unhappy with themselves that they go overboard trying to change their image; sometimes the changes make no sense. I know a young man who was raised rich. Besides a beautiful home in Manhattan, his family had summer and winter vacation homes. He traveled extensively as a youngster and grew up in a world of nannies, tutors, and private schools. He graduated cum laude from an Ivy League university, but if you met him on the street, you'd think he was a grade school dropout from Hell's Kitchen. His army surplus wardrobe and his language, which seemed dominated by the seven words not allowed on network television, became his trademarks. Thanks to family connections, he always held a responsible position (lots of them); but he consciously packaged himself to shock those who knew his background and disarm others with his intelligence and knowledge. He loved being a paradox—like TV tough guy Robert Blake surprising his audience with a soliloquy from *Macbeth,* or dopey-sounding Gomer Pyle stunning everyone by singing light opera. Although his facade was transparent and was generally treated as an idiosyncrasy and shrugged off, it certainly confused one's first impression of him.

Over a period of six weeks, I had several phone conversations with a woman who worked for a company I was doing business with. Although I had never seen her, I had conjured up an image of her based on the sound of her voice, her manner of speech, and her choice of words. Compared to her, I thought, the Wicked Witch of the West must be a raving beauty. I hated to phone her. Her voice was unpleasantly high and strained, and she spoke in a clipped staccato monotone. She never wasted a word or missed a beat. I fantasized that she was speaking to me from a phone booth and that there was a line of angry people pounding on the door and shouting for her to get off. After every conversation, I shouted into the phone, "You couldn't work for me for five minutes!" (Of course, she had already hung up.) Finally, I met this woman and I simply could not reconcile what I saw with what I heard. She was extremely attractive, the kind of woman who can make the day for a girl-watcher. Her voice was the same as on the phone: clipped, hurried, and intense, yet disinterested. Over a cup of coffee in her office, I learned that her style was really contrived. She was trying to project an image of no-nonsense efficiency. Resolved not to be perceived as the office centerfold, she had built this wall of ice around her. She succeeded in diminishing the importance of her good looks, but she wasn't being perceived as serious, businesslike, and efficient. Her uptight demeanor made her seem fragile, brittle, and on the edge of hysteria. She put herself in a defensive position and sent out unpleasant messages that distorted and sullied the image she was trying to present.

Most affectations are transparent and advertise your personal dissatisfaction. We all know people who pick up accents, fad phrases, and mannerisms like quick-change artists or chameleons. I remember a wonderful woman who returned to New York after a four-week business trip in London sounding more like the Queen of England than Elizabeth herself. In one month she had transformed her lovely midwestern sound into a royal caricature. She eventually gave it up, but until then she certainly was sending out some strange messages about herself.

We don't need to become illusionists to evoke the kind of response we want from others. Without pretense or mimicry, we can overcome what makes us uncomfortable with ourselves. It may take a little more time and effort, but the results will be worthwhile.

Just remember this: Once you open your mouth and start talking, your listener begins to dissect you: analyzing, categorizing, characterizing, and judging. It's incredible how much can get jammed into a first impression. Give someone a couple of minutes of your time and he'll "know" whether or not you're intelligent, educated, warm, and friendly, or cold and self-centered; creative and courageous, a sure winner, or a born loser. He or she may be totally off base, but most of what goes into his judgment mill are the personal messages you send out.

6

Motivating Others: The Basic Tools

I f your career has reached a plateau even though you have the desire and the ability to keep climbing, it could be a problem of motivating other people.

You're in better shape than most people if you're in a field you like and are knowledgeable, skilled, and self-motivated. You certainly have the edge over anyone who lacks your positive qualities. If you're a self-starter who knows what you want to achieve and can keep focused on your goals, balancing your time and your priorities toward that end, the odds in your favor are further improved. Still, I know people, lots of them, who have the skills, the knowledge, and the drive to succeed, but fall short anyway—short, that is, of their own aspirations and expectations. They may have some measure of success, but don't reach the level of achievement they're capable of. They feel slowed down or "short-circuited," not because of their lack of talent or experience, but because of what they perceive to be bureaucratic roadblocks or people problems.

Like it or not, much of our success depends on the skills and motivation of other people; so unless you're an artist, a craftsman, or a professional who operates independently, you had better understand and develop strong *people management* skills. If you require help to promote and implement your ideas—whether it's getting your budget approved, translating your sketches into models, or keeping your files organized and available—you must recognize the relative importance of each person involved. You must consciously work at developing and maintaining *appropriate* relationships to positively affect the behavior and performance of others and at times to influence them to do, feel, or think the way you want.

Some people feel uncomfortable with the idea of consciously trying to influence others' behavior. To them, the concept connotes imposition, coercion, and unwarranted and unwanted pressure. Of course, there are plenty of insensitive people who take advantage of and corrupt others with their persuasive motivational skills—confidence men, child seducers, power-crazed individuals like Jim Jones, Qaddafi, and Hitler.

We've all been exercising our motivational powers since birth, when we first screamed for our dinner and complained about the discomfort of a wet diaper. Whenever we're engaged in any personal contact, we're almost certain to be practicing our motivational skills or reacting to someone else's. It's the normal and natural way of getting things done: communicating, relating, and getting along with others. There's nothing wrong with it. What's wrong is that although we've been practicing the art our entire lives, so many of us aren't very skilled at it.

JUST GETTING ALONG
ISN'T ENOUGH

Being popular is as ego-enhancing to an adult in the workplace as it is to a youngster in school. But it isn't the key to a successful career. I know a lot of people who get along just fine with everyone they associate with, but they do it the easy way. They humbly acquiesce to almost any suggestion and people love to have them around. They become instinctive gofers. They go for the coffee before they're asked. They indiscriminately share anyone's enthusiasm. When they have a good idea, they give it away without any expectation of even sharing in its proprietorship. They're popular, all right!

A sales director once boasted to me that one of his reps was voted Most Popular Salesperson for three straight years at a regional convention hosted by their industry's retailers.

"Congratulations," I said, "but why did they choose him?"

"He's a terrific person and will do anything for you. He has a great personality and a great sense of humor. I'd have been surprised if he hadn't won."

"Is he your most productive salesperson?" I asked.

"No."

"One of your top five?"

"No."

"Near the bottom?"

"Yes."

When he dug out the salesman's call reports, "just for the heck of it," a couple of items almost jumped off the summary page. One, the guy's entertainment costs were extraordinarily high. Two, he led his district in nonsale calls—that is, he frequently reported: "Had appointment, but buyer was too busy to go over the line; will see tomorrow."

No wonder this guy won a popularity contest! He wined, dined, and entertained his customers and allowed them to put him off whenever it was convenient for them to do so. He made life easy for them and got nothing in return but their ballot. That might have been okay if they were voting him a raise or a bonus, but they weren't. He knew how to get along with his customers, all right, but not to his advantage or to theirs, either.

Getting along with people in a way that strengthens and enhances your position takes as much thought, skill, and practice as any science taught in the schools and universities.

Dale Carnegie, whose self-help empire is built on the premise that dealing with people is man's most difficult challenge, said: "Even in such technical lines as engineering, about 15 percent of one's financial success is due to one's technical knowledge and about 85 percent is due to skill in human engineering—to personality and the ability to lead people." So far as I'm concerned, there's no reason to argue with Carnegie's numbers. Whatever the percentages, the point is certainly true that there's a strong correlation between a person's success (not only financial) and his or her people management skills.

PEOPLE MANAGEMENT SKILLS

It's easy to recognize those folks who have finely developed people management skills. They usually get their way (whether it's choosing a restaurant, a supplier, or a relocation site), *and their associates either are happy to follow them or aren't aware of being led.*

The most successful motivators often become the most successful leaders. They are the people who make things happen. They move others to action with their ability to influence, inspire, and nurture. They stimulate others, spark them, move them, and arouse them, through encouragement, nourishment, and inducement. They're persuasive, knowing when to apply pressure, and what kind to use—the carrot or the prod. I'm not talking about bullies. Anyone can move another to action with a gun or a whip, but I don't consider such a person a possessor of people management skills.

I'm most impressed with seemingly ordinary people who

have the extraordinary ability to motivate others to strive for a superior performance without sinking psychological hooks into them that rob them of their individuality or self-worth. Many successful motivators come across as being outgoing and charismatic; some may seem manipulative at times, but all have an instinctive ability to make themselves understood and to understand the words, feelings, and actions of others. They're also able to draw out of others the meanings of their words and actions. In short, they are skilled communicators.

What are the skills the most successful motivators possess?

1. The ability to think clearly—to separate the facts from the suppositions, the wishes, and the fictions—and to think objectively, keeping emotions and biases in check. Skilled motivators know what they want to accomplish and are able to keep goals and motives uncluttered and uncomplicated, even when they are dealing with highly charged emotional or political issues.

They differentiate between desirability and necessity, always trying to keep their priorities in order and in balance.

2. The ability to make themselves understood. When a successful motivator expresses his ideas and feelings—to an individual or to a group—his words, tone, and body language are in harmony, never sending out conflicting and confusing messages.

Motivators talk the language of the listener, taking no chance that their points will be lost because of a language barrier. They do this without patronizing the other person.

Successful motivators carefully read the reactions of the person they are trying to influence, and know when they're on target or missing the mark.

They realize that most people have poor listening skills, and strive to make their points in the most direct, comprehensible way possible. It's a fact that most people only remember twenty percent of what they hear.

3. Effective motivators are skilled listeners. They listen for reactions to make sure that they are understood, and listen to understand the position of the other person. They listen for any clues or hints that give insights into the other's position. They are as conscious of the other person's choice of words, tone, and body language as they are of their own. What the other person is saying truly interests them.

Apparently, what they do is not easy. *If it were, a lot more of us would be good listeners!* Here are a couple of things that separate the really skilled listener from the competition. (*a*) They pay attention to what the other person is saying—that is, they shut out most distractions and stay tuned in to the other person. (*b*) Their greatest feat is to keep their own mind in check: to keep it from wandering or racing ahead or using the other person's talking time to prepare for their next opportunity to speak.

4. Successful motivators are skilled conversationalists. I mean they know how to exchange thoughts and feelings. They know the difference between conversing and lecturing or preaching. Like a good ballroom dancer, the skilled conversationalist can lead his partner without seeming manipulative or coercive. Because they are listening carefully, they are able to keep the other person from digressing too far from the subject. With a smile, an exclamation, or a short appropriate comment or question, they steer the conversation; and at the same time, the speaker feels he has an appreciative audience. The other person feels not only comfortable, safe, and flattered but, most important, more communicative.

As far as I'm concerned, conversation is the most effective and reliable of all motivational formats. It has to be. It's the most direct and the most flexible.

110

5. The most effective motivator is also skilled at written communication. For some people, it's easier and safer to put thoughts down on paper than express them orally. That's certainly understandable. The writer has the time to pick and choose his words, to systematically lay out his thoughts without being diverted or distracted by the recipient's reactions, and to say no more or no less than he intends. The really good communicator does more than just transmit his message. He has the ability to project his voice and personality onto the written page to create a proper mood and evoke a response.

He also manages to keep the time factor in perspective and gets his message across at the most opportune time. Timing can be a very delicate factor when you're dealing with emotional or hot issues in a letter or memo. For example, I think it's unfair and counterproductive to drop a highly critical letter on an employee just before he starts a vacation; and a good communicator makes sure that the feelings and sentiments he expresses in a letter that is written on Wednesday will be valid the following Monday, when the letter is received and read.

So topflight motivators—whether they're influencing their children, their customers, their constituency, or their employees—are skilled listeners and expressers. Of course, it takes more than just communication skills to consistently motivate others.

ARE EFFECTIVE COMMUNICATORS
JUST LUCKY?

Most of the observations in this book are based on a thirty-five-year career that has focused on communication and motivation, but they're not the conclusions of any statistical studies and can't be documented scientifically. So from my experience, to the question "Are effective communicators just lucky?" I'd answer, "Almost always!"

They may have been lucky to be born into talking, articulate families that encouraged free and open discussions and even arguments. They were especially lucky if they were raised in an environment where it was possible to express their feelings without shame or fear, and where a premium was put on nonverbal as well as verbal articulation.

Sadly, not many of us were taught communication skills—not in school and not by trained professionals. Those of us who had a natural talent for self-expression might have been guided into student politics, the debating team, the drama club, or the school newspaper—all good stuff. But the rest—the shy, the insecure, the awkward communicators—were rarely, if ever, considered likely candidates for the extracurricular activities that could help develop their talents.

It really bothers me that our schools and colleges do not consider communication skills to be as important as physical education or European history. It puzzles me that the admission requirements of many colleges and universities include proficiency in a foreign language but do not require that one be able to articulate thoughts and ideas in a comprehensible way in conversational English.

I'm not a long-odds gambler and I consider it ridiculous that we leave to luck the development of our skills to communicate effectively. All of us, in and out of business, need the skills to make ourselves understood: to accurately describe our feelings, report our findings, state our positions, argue our points of view, ask for help, or plead for support. We need the skills to make sense out of the messages that are forever bombarding our senses. Communication skills are as critical as any others and they should be taught to us from elementary school on.

112

THE THREE R'S AREN'T ENOUGH

Our schools are having more than their share of problems turning out students who can read, write, and do basic arithmetic. The problems are severe and alarming, as anyone dealing with young job applicants can tell you.

Many of our high school graduates are functionally illiterate—and some make it through college in spite of this deficiency. I understand that most college textbooks today are written at a junior high school level.

People who have difficulty reading have a terrible time writing, so you can imagine what's happening to the art of written communication. It can be an unnerving experience to go through a mailbag of letters written by business people who are trying to straighten out a shipping foul-up, are questioning an invoice or a discount, or are asking for information. The quality of the writing is often childlike and confusing; the spelling and grammar errors are minor problems compared to the writer's inability to simply organize and express his or her thoughts. Most customer service people need the skills of a cryptographer to get through the letters. In addition, many people who are paid to untangle customer problems add to the confusion because of their inability to write in a clear, straightforward fashion.

Arithmetic? The remedial math classes in our colleges and universities are packed with young men and women who graduated from high school without understanding the basics of mathematics.

A young registered nurse told me that although she successfully completed all her science courses and got her degree from a prestigious school, she didn't know her multiplication tables! Perhaps the widespread use of electronic calculators

113

and personal computers may be a contributing factor but not to that degree.

A high school graduate who was hired by a large company as a file clerk eventually applied for a position in a department that dealt primarily with statistics and got the job. An hour after he began his new assignment, he appeared at the door of his supervisor's office, looking confused and dejected.

"It's these percentages. It's crazy, but I don't remember how to calculate them."

His new boss swallowed hard, knowing that somebody in personnel had screwed up, but he didn't want to add to the young man's discomfort, so he worked a simple problem for him. "We had 1200 units of catalog item 11230 in inventory and shipped 150 units. To find out what percentage of the inventory was shipped, divide 150 by 1200. You get .125, so 12.5 percent of the inventory was shipped."

The young man looked at the numbers his boss had scribbled on the scratch pad and groaned, "Oh, no; not long division, decimals, and fractions! You don't need me, you need Einstein!"

I didn't make these stories up. Educators know this is a serious problem, and they're trying to do something about it. I'm convinced that if personal communication skills were taught in our schools, there would be a dramatic improvement in most of the other subjects.

We need courses in listening—not hearing, but *listening for meaning.* Poor listening skills must cost business and industry millions of dollars annually, not to mention its cost in terms of damaged and shattered interpersonal relationships.

We need courses in the techniques and mechanics of successful conversation. It's as important and rewarding as any skill one might possess. We need courses that will encourage and teach us from childhood on to express ourselves in writing and to communicate orally.

There are things that can be done today to improve our communication skills. First, though, we have to recognize and admit that they need improving. Sometimes that's difficult to do, because we often blame other people for our miscommunications. It's easy and comfortable to believe that others are at fault for misunderstanding our words and meanings—that they don't listen, don't concentrate, and distort our meanings with their own perceptions. Well, they probably do contribute to the problem, but the chances are, so do we.

Over the years, the communication problem has been addressed in a variety of ways, and at times, it has been mass-marketed to the public. Some programs have been enormously successful and are continuously available; others come on like a fad and disappear; and some take on the characteristics of an underground cult.

The Dale Carnegie Courses are still available and offer effective programs that deal with relating and communicating with others.

Transactional Analysis groups have been on the scene for years, and the method's key texts, including *I'm OK—You're OK*, are still best-selling books.

The P.E.T. (Parent Effectiveness Training) program, though focused on parent-children problems, has a practical approach to active listening that is helpful for anyone in any relationship.

I recommend the Toastmasters Club to anyone who has qualms about speaking to large groups. Another new and worthwhile program involves seminars on the art of negotiation.

You can benefit from any of the above suggestions, but the very best way to develop your speaking skills is through practical experience. No matter what job you're in, put yourself in front of an audience whenever you can, and it needn't be a business situation. Speak up at PTA, church, and town meetings. Volunteer for committee and task force assignments where you have to present ideas and information. Speak in schools, clubs, and social groups—to any organization that is interested in your work and experience. There are plenty of opportunities for everyone who wants to hone his or her communication skills.

Don't run off to one of those groups, though, until you read the remaining chapters of this book. They may be all you need to become an efficient listener and a proficient expresser.

7

Motivating Others: A Leader's Responsibility

W hether you're trying to mo- tivate an individual, a small group, or a crowd, the basics—respect, recognition, and reward—are the same. The dynamics are different and so are some of the techniques, but in every case it's an important, exciting, and challenging experience. I spend a great deal of my time trying to motivate groups of people, and I love it. It's exciting when an audience of several hundred people gives me a standing ovation and I leave the auditorium feeling that my message really made a difference. But it doesn't top the gratification of watching the blossoming career of someone I've worked with one-on-one. Nor is it any more exciting than working with a small task force or a committee, moving its members to translate ideas into products or sales and helping them attain new levels of achievement.

Motivating another to attain success is anything but an act of altruism. If you're an executive or in management, your success depends on how effective a motivator you are. You're judged not only on your own performance but on the performance of the team—the task force, department, or division—that you are responsible for.

I spent most of my adult life working for a company that expected nothing short of a top performance from each of its employees. I was ultimately responsible for seeing that thousands of those employees met their objectives and turned in winning performances. My success depended on their success and I never forgot it.

Some people believe that all that matters is getting the job done. I don't agree. Of course, it's important to get the product to the marketplace, the manuscript into production, or the system into place, but it's also important that the assignments provide an arena and an environment where careers are nurtured by leaders who motivate their people to strive for their best possible performance. Everybody involved should benefit. It's not enough if only the leaders and the stockholders gain. Properly motivated people will feel a sense of achievement—of being a fundamental part of the total picture. The individuals who get the work done should feel proud and pleased with their performance. They will then be eager and energized for the next assignment.

To motivate others you must think and behave like a leader. Your actions and words will help others to reach higher levels of achievement with the opportunity and the freedom to grow.

To be a true leader and motivator, you have to come to grips with your feelings about delegating responsibility. You cannot lead effectively if you refuse to relinquish some of your authority. You must accept the fact that an ambitious person who isn't given responsibility will not be stimulated and moved for long. In my book *The IBM Way*, I said this:

> You can't talk about leadership without talking about responsibility and accountability; as far as I'm concerned, you can't separate the two. A leader must delegate responsibility and provide the freedom to make decisions, and then be held accountable for the results. It seems simple enough, but leadership often

runs into roadblocks right from the outset. Frequently it's the fault of the person who delegates. That's because he does it with his fingers crossed. He goes through the ritual of delegating but he just can't let go. Perhaps he has second thoughts about the decision, or maybe he's afraid that he's weakened his own power base. Whatever the reason, he intends to keep an eye on things. Soon he is breathing down the neck of his newly appointed manager, scrutinizing every action, criticizing every decision, allowing little or no room for expression or experiment. He renders his manager helpless and then holds him accountable for the results. The poor guy doesn't have a chance. He stops trying to be innovative, and by not exercising his authority, returns the decision-making to his boss. He becomes an implementer, which is probably what he was before his promotion. The people who work under this manager know that he's powerless—and they resent it. They want to work for a winner. His promotion may have added something to his paycheck, but it can never be enough for what it cost him in self-esteem and peace of mind. He was a victim of the "captain of the ship" syndrome, in which the person at the top assumes all the responsibility.

There are times when the opposite occurs. A person is given the responsibility, authority and freedom to get a job done, but is never held accountable. A business can be driven into the ground because a leader recklessly delegates responsibility as if he were getting rid of a hot potato, then detaches himself from the delegate and his decisions. It catches up with him eventually, when a crisis surfaces that he can't avoid. This kind of leader doesn't want to be held accountable, but somehow doesn't hold the other person accountable either. It seems impossible, doesn't it? But it happens somewhere every day. Personally, I want to be held accountable and responsible for whatever decisions I have the freedom and authority to make and to implement.

Effective leadership thus becomes the underpinning for the following nine bases that have to be touched by anyone who hopes to successfully motivate another person.

THE BASIC STEPS
TO BEING A LEADER

1. Establish who's in charge. Remember these things: *(a)* The people you're trying to motivate have to believe that you have more leverage in the company than they have. They have to accept you as an authority figure whose influence can help or hurt them. *(b)* You want people to trust you and believe what you say. They should feel confident that you will deliver whatever you promise and that you are fair, understanding, helpful, and compassionate. *(c)* There's nothing wrong with those you are leading being cognizant of your position, but they must respect you for your integrity and your ability, and that doesn't come with a title—it has to be earned. *(d)* Avoid mentor-protégé relationships. Too many young people right off college campuses and some ambitious young turks in business have the notion that the surest road to success is one that's walked hand in hand with a sponsor. This gives the person starting a career the unhealthy idea that politics has the advantage over performance. The mentor-protégé association may work in a profession or an art such as wood carving, where a master's knowledge and skill are so esoteric that they're not attainable any other way. But I haven't been in a business situation that fits that criterion.

Whenever I've been approached by aggressive young people who wanted me to be their mentor and sponsor, I refused on the grounds that, one, it would add a dimension to our relationship that would shift too much responsibility for their success on my shoulders and, two, it would give them a false sense of security. *(e)* Don't confuse your role as leader with that of friend. It's important to have pleasant, cordial working relationships but always remain businesslike. I know leaders who find themselves in a morass of confusion and discomfort because they want to be "loved" by the people they manage. I always believed that the people under my leadership deserved to have the best manager possible, and that's what I tried to be. They didn't need me to be their friend, nor did I need them to be mine. Mutual respect is the basis for the ideal working relationship. Also, it is imperative for proper motivation. Friendships may develop, but should not be the goal a leader strives for. A great leader is loved because he is respected. It never works the other way.

2. Know what you want to accomplish. Define your goals, short term and long term. Then put them down on paper. Refer to them often. Review and amend them when you must. Be a planner. Develop a strategy for accomplishing those goals and a calendar of checkpoints so you can monitor your progress and make sure that you're moving ahead. Consider putting down on paper in the morning what you want to accomplish that day, in priority sequence, then critique your performance. Did you do those things that were most important, or did you spend your time less productively? The way you organize your time and balance it against your priorities should be a model for those you want to motivate. If you're floundering, you can't be much of an inspiration to someone else. Telegraph that you're unsure of your direction and the person who relies on you is certain to feel insecure and

123

alarmed. You need more than a vague sense of what you want to accomplish and how you're going to do it.

3. Know what you want each person you manage to accomplish. Set specific goals for a person to achieve—something you can refer to and monitor. If you don't do this, your evaluation of him or her will fluctuate and be distorted. Unless you gauge another person's performance against your expectations, you won't be able to give very much motivational help. Too many leaders get in trouble by judging people on style: the energy they expend, the enthusiasm they project, their seriousness, and the perception of them by others. These are all important, but successful careers are built on achievement, not style. It's up to you, the leader, to separate the two. You can't do that if you haven't defined your expectations and goals for people's performance.

4. Let him know what you expect. Don't keep him guessing! Too many leaders treat the people they're supposed to be motivating as though they are mind readers or psychics. Face the person eyeball to eyeball and spell out what you feel that individual needs to do to improve his performance and career possibilities.

I recall a promising executive who lost the handle on his career because he never really understood what he needed to do to move ahead. He was put in the situation of always trying to outguess his boss, who never communicated his expectations. In time, this talented, once action-oriented young executive became a gun-shy, indecisive yes-man. That's not what the boss wanted, but he played a major role in shaping this disappointing career.

No one who ever worked for me had to wonder what I expected of him or had to wait for an annual performance appraisal to find out. Nor is it necessary to limit the formal

124

appraisal to once a year. Successful leaders and motivators have an ongoing dialogue with their people, letting them know what is expected and what might happen when expectations are met or exceeded and what might happen if they're not. They reiterate their ideas in a memo so there will be no misunderstanding about it later.

I can't stress enough the importance of this issue.

Let a person you manage know what you think of his performance. Don't let him wonder whether or not you're satisfied. If you've done a good job of clarifying your expectations and worked out a performance plan that's monitored throughout the year, it's no problem keeping him apprised of his progress. No problem, that is, if you've kept an open line of communication.

5. Find out what your employee wants for himself. Insist that he articulate his goals, aspirations, and expectations. You need to know if you're both on the same wavelength. If his expectations are unrealistic, tell him so. Don't hedge or lead him on. This is a very serious problem. If you make a judgment about a person's potential that puts a ceiling on the level he might reach in the company, it should be shared with the employee. If it's not shared, you're certain to collide somewhere down the road, and it will be a problem when it happens. It's possible that if you discover your differences early enough, the employee will accept the judgment as appropriate and be motivated to change.

The greatest value of exploring your employee's expectations is that you're giving him the opportunity to express his ideas and feelings. *Everybody enjoys talking about himself, and thinks well of anyone who's interested in listening.*

6. Find out what your employee expects of you. It's important to know what the person you're trying to affect expects in terms of managerial help and managerial interference. If he's reluctant to tell you or seems to be holding back, let him know where you stand on delegating responsibility, stepping in when things appear to go wrong, and promoting from within. Do what you can to draw him out. You may discover that he expects a great deal more guidance than you thought necessary; or step-by-step approval, something you might consider redundant and a misuse of your time. If he expects regular meetings with you—weekly, or monthly—you should know it. If he feels that to perform his job properly he needs more autonomy than you're prepared to give, you should know that too.

The point is that just as your expectations must be articulated and understood by people you manage, so must their expectations of you be expressed and understood. The more open the discussions, the less chance there will be of confusion and grief when things are hectic and there's no time to establish the ground rules.

7. Take being a role model seriously. I don't go along with a leader who maintains, "Do as I say, not as I do." It's a foolish attitude, but more important, it doesn't work. If you're in a leadership position, your behavior has a tremendous impact on the behavior of the people you manage. I don't mean the way they react to your suggestions and directives; I mean the way they react to one another and to outsiders—co-workers, customers, and your management. You're probably more influential than you think. Your personality, mood swings, and worries, for example, have a subliminal effect on others. Visit a department headed by a surly-tempered, selfish person, and it won't be long before you feel the tension and the anger, even when he's not there. Conversely, if the leader is frightened, weak, and unsure of himself, the futility in his department hangs in the air like a cold chill. It's also true, thank goodness, that if the department head is relaxed, self-assured, good-humored, and enthusiastic, his positive attitude will give a lift and a positive resonance to his department or office.

Once you're in a managerial position, you're a role model, like it or not. If you have no calendar integrity, don't expect your people to come to work on time, keep appointments, return phone calls, or respond to mail promptly. If you're a gossip, leak confidences, and complain vehemently about your bosses, don't expect confidentiality and loyalty from the people who report to you. If you're an unorganized procrastinator, don't be disappointed if your people are confused and sloppy. You set the tone and the pace, you control the energy level, you define the ethics, you impart to your people the importance and seriousness of what they and you do.

8. Expect others to be self-motivated, but don't count on it. I'm not implying there aren't plenty of self-starters in the workplace. There are. But the motivation level of even the high achievers fluctuates, and the swings can be dramatic. Don't ever underestimate the importance of the motivational factor when you're initiating any program or plan.

You're a leader and it's your responsibility to the people you manage—and the company you work for—to motivate others to improve, to grow, and to flourish. If you're going to keep improving your own situation, you have to get others to produce more, waste less, and be more innovative. You want them to reach and s-t-r-e-t-c-h, but why should they stretch for you?

9. Understand that the quality of your leadership is determined by the methods you use to motivate others. I've stressed the need for open, honest, and sensitive, yet freewheeling, communication and, in a sense, laid down the rules of fairness in the motivation game. Unfortunately, the world is loaded with leaders who reject the idea that motivation is an issue to be pondered or given much consideration. I remember meeting with a group of sales managers to discuss the subject of motivation and incentives. Each person was responsible for a national sales force that sold a product line directly to retail accounts throughout the country.

"What's the most effective motivational tool you have at your disposal?" I asked.

The first response came without a moment's hesitation.

"Keeping their jobs," one of the young managers blurted out. "I let my staff know from day one that every day, they put their job on the line. If they don't produce, they're out! That's the most powerful incentive I can think of. They know that there's plenty of salespeople looking for good jobs."

A leader with this attitude can quickly undermine the value of a "good" job. The threat of being fired hanging over one's head is an incentive, all right—it's an incentive for an employee to figure out how little he can do to avoid the cut while exploring other career options. Useful motivational tools don't exacerbate turnover, or burn out an employee. They're designed to generate enthusiasm and build loyalty.

It's easy to get people to work harder and faster if you put guns to their heads or whips to their backs and quickly get rid of those who resist or are unable to respond. That's the way the slave drivers did it. Unfortunately, it was somewhat effective, but it wasn't right. Today, there are many leaders and managers who motivate their people with similar techniques. They don't use a gun or a whip, but they try to get things done with threats and coercion, by degrading and dehumanizing. "Run Scared" is their slogan. They don't break backs or heads, but they do break spirits. I find these leaders detestable.

Their primary mode of influencing another person is with the threat of punishment. They are the bullies who, as far as I'm concerned, have no place in business, the school, or the home, but they are everywhere. They often operate on the edge of hysteria, have fragile egos, and seem to get pleasure out of hurting the most defenseless employee. Many of them turn out to be all roar and no bite, and once found out, they're relegated to the role of evil-tongued buffoon by the people they're supposed to be motivating. Managers who operate in this mode are a dangerous and serious handicap to any legitimate firm. In the short term, their tactics seem to drive their employees to work harder and more intensely, but it doesn't take much scrutiny to realize that under the facade of "hard work," less real productivity is accomplished; and you can be certain that little creative energy is expended.

Leaders who believe that "driving herd" is a successful method of motivation are foolish. The damage they do to their employees' pride and morale is brutal and slow to repair. It's a wonder to me that companies that occupy the most modern buildings and are equipped with the most sophisticated machinery tolerate managers and supervisors whose styles of operation are outdated and dangerous.

Don't get the idea from what I just said that I never blow my top or hurt anybody's feelings. Though I know that an employee (or anyone) who has his dignity and pride will be more responsive to the kind of motivation I advocate, I realize that if you're in a leadership position—executive, managerial, or supervisory—there are times when you have to pull your rank. Like it or not, part of your motivational power is the leverage you have to discipline or demote someone.

As in any society where rules and regulations are established to help things run smoothly and fairly, those holding leadership positions in a company must, at times, act as judge, police officer, and parent. Rules and regulations that are not implemented and supported lose their meaning. More important, they confuse and demoralize the employees who abide by them when they know that those who break the rules pay no dues for the transgression. I believe that rules, like laws, should be reviewed periodically, with the unnecessary or outdated ones stricken from the books. No one should blindly follow orders they don't understand; therefore, those that can't be explained and justified should be dropped. However, a company's principles never become outdated and must be protected. No leader should turn his back on or shrug off a violation of the company's declared code of ethics or tolerate an employee's abuse of a customer, another employee, or anyone else. I don't like to use the term "punishment," but in these cases, I'd come down hard on any offender.

On the other hand, I don't believe in punishing a person for making a single mistake as long as it's not a violation of ethics and morality. I've seen too many instances where leaders treat errors as though they were crimes. Their staff are afraid of making a decision without prior approval to protect themselves. That's hardly the way to encourage a person to take on responsibility and build self-esteem. We all goof at times, and when we do, we suffer enough without our bosses piling it on. It's another story, of course, if the errors become chronic. The error-prone person may need some counseling, additional training, or maybe a pink slip.

For some reason, most of us can be demotivators without any textbooks or classroom training. We instinctively know the use of tantrums, threats, and insults, especially when we're not afraid of the repercussions. We get results, all right, but in the long run, they're not what we want. I have the reputation of being a topflight motivator, of getting people to perform without degrading them—better than that, of getting them to perform gladly. I'm convinced that what works for me and what I've seen work for others will work for anyone who's willing to try it. What follows won't be a review of an introductory psych course. I never turned to Pavlov or Skinner for help in trying to motivate another person. What I know about the art of inciting others to improve their performance and stretch their potential came from working with the likes of IBM's Watsons (father and son). I also held positions that forced me to think "motivation" from morning until night, day in, day out, for years. Most recently, I'm energized by working with some of the most motivated people I've ever met in a variety of industries.

8

Motivating Others with Money and Things

E veryone knows that money is one of the major motivators in the world. Happily for the human race, it's not the number one driving force in the lives of most of us, even though, at times, it may seem so. (Later, I'll discuss what I consider the greatest motivators.) Of course, money is one of the most important reasons a person is willing to work eight or more hours a day. No one knows that better than business people. That's why it's bewildering to me that so many companies ignore the incentive factor when they develop their employees' compensation packages. To explain what I mean, I'll discuss the various components that make up most pay packages.

SALARY ONLY

A fixed or generated salary will not motivate an individual for very long, or stimulate him to raise his performance level or increase his productivity. The salary range may be predetermined for each job description with increments within the range tied to such things as education, experience, and perhaps longevity. The problem is that a person's base pay is primarily connected to his position, not to his performance.

Initially a person in a new position will demonstrate his dedication and enthusiasm. He will prove to the company that he's worth the salary they're paying him. Unfortunately, it doesn't take long for an employee to get used to his salary and realize that the quality of his work has little to do with the size of his paycheck. He stops making a connection between salary and performance and even salary and position and accepts the notion that what he's really being paid for is his time—regardless of how he spends it. For the most part, he can either work hard or goof off and the paycheck comes through unchanged.

What you end up with is employees working in an environment that fosters disinterest and mediocrity.

Salary grids are often misused and become a demotivating factor. Most corporations intend the salary grids as guidelines. However, many managers hide behind them to avoid giving someone an earned but higher than usual raise. I've known of cases where managers lost good employees because they pretended the salary grid was the manifestation of an inflexible law. In another unfortunate situation, a superior applicant was rejected because his demands were a few dollars more than the grid permitted.

Good managers give unusually high raises when it is warranted and no raise at all when one isn't deserved.

The salary becomes less motivational when wages and raises are negotiated by the employee's union and a committee appointed by the company. The employee knows that you, his manager, has little input in the resolution of his income, and as far as I'm concerned, that's not healthy.

This kind of system often discourages an employee's allegiance to his company and to his manager; after all, every time a contract expires, the union, not his boss, is perceived to champion the employee's cause. It's a system that all too often encourages those who really depend on one another to become adversaries.

I can't think of any situation where straight salary alone is the ideal way to compensate an employee, but it's still important that the salary part of any compensation package be treated with a great deal of thought and sensitivity.

I disagree with those who believe it's good business to have employees clawing just to make ends meet. When a person can't stretch his check to cover basic needs (food, clothing, housing, transportation), it's fear and desperation, not motivation, that govern his performance.

It's important to consider a job applicant's specific needs before you hire him. I wouldn't employ a person who requires more money to meet his fixed obligations than I'm able to offer. He may be perfect for the job and want the position so badly that he's willing to take it in hope that once he's started, he can convince you to pay him more money. His enthusiasm for the job and your enthusiasm for him are certain to deaden after a paycheck or two, when he's getting deeper in debt and begins to pressure you for a premature salary increase.

I think that any good manager knows it's as important to put a reasonable dollar value on a position as it is to price a product properly. It reveals how you feel about the importance of the job and the person who fills it. If you want a new employee's respect and productivity, it's imperative that you be up-front about the company's policies regarding salary and raises. If raises are given annually and no sooner, say so. Let a person know what the salary potential is for the position he's filling and what factors determine the size of the raise. *Don't promise anything you can't deliver.*

It's the company's responsibility to present its pay package in the most creative way possible—so long as the presentation is honest not only in the way it's defined but in what's implied or inferred. What services a company expects to "buy" for the wages it pays should be spelled out in specific terms from the outset. That's one reason I'm thoroughly sold on IBM's policy that a new employee must be hired by the person who will be his or her manager, not a recruiting team or a personnel director. The manager responsible and accountable for the new employee's performance is in a position to say, "Look, I know what you expect to receive in your paycheck every two weeks. This is what I will expect you to do to earn it. I promise that I'll deliver, so long as you deliver."

Salary becomes a sensitive issue when one employee finds out that another employee doing the same work with the same responsibilities is earning more money. The issue becomes more sensitive when the complaining employee knows that the quality of his work is superior to the other's. In straight salary jobs, longevity usually accounts for the difference, so there's no way for the newer employee to catch up. Experience, loyalty, and staying power are important, but at some point, there should be a salary adjustment that demonstrates a belief in equal work, equal pay—a true meritocracy.

Companies that have the reputation for paying well have little trouble keeping their pipeline of applicants full. If they offer no additional money incentives or only token incentives, they lose the people with entrepreneurial spirit and many of the wild ducks.

RAISES

The raise should be a carrot that management can use to motivate and reward its employees. It's a tremendous loss and frustration to those responsible for increasing productivity (and to the most productive employees) when the raise is mandated by contract.

138

I'm against contracted raises of any kind, including cost-of-living increases and guaranteed minimum across-the-board raises. That doesn't make me anti-worker. I was an employee for thirty-four years, and a substantial part of my income was salary. Raises were important, but I never wanted anyone to negotiate a raise for me; I wanted to earn it. Although at times I worked as a member of a team, I never wanted to be judged by the accomplishments of the group. I wanted to be looked at as an individual, judged by my contributions, and rewarded after a fair evaluation.

When a person comes to grips with the idea that the salary increase he receives has little or nothing to do with his performance and accepts the fact that it's either a company give-away or a plum won by a labor negotiating team, his incentive to work is bound to plateau or take a nosedive.

It's ridiculous to give anyone a raise that's not perform-ance connected, and it's totally bananas to give someone a raise who doesn't deserve it. Across-the-board raises benefit no one but the nondeserving and cheat those who deserve a big-ger piece of the pie. The amount of money that can be budg-eted for salary increases is finite. The more you give to the bottom twenty percent of your people, the less you have for the top twenty percent. I've heard of people who were on "warning" because of poor performance when their pay-checks were fattened by a programmed raise. It makes no sense, and it's not fair.

If you're stuck with a straight salary system—that is, if your company won't (or can't) pay true incentives like commis-sions, profit sharing, and bonuses—then I suggest that you fight to end the annual fixed raise.

Even if your system of issuing raises is a good one—that is, it's directly connected to performance—you lose a lot of the incentive value by passing out the increases only once a year.

First, it's almost impossible to be motivated in February by the possibility of a pay raise in December. Six months is long enough to expect anyone to wait for recognition, especially if a salary increase is the only reward he's apt to get. The person who's dragging his feet is more likely to perk up if he finds out halfway into the year that he missed out on a decent raise but has a chance to recoup some of it. Second, there's a tendency by a lot of managers to write off an employee's inferior work when it occurs in the first part of the year. If the person improves toward year end, his manager may recommend a raise that reflects a year's good work. Some employees are cognizant of this, and act like the apartment doorman who doesn't give the tenant the time of day from January through November but smothers him with thoughtfulness and graciousness in December—at least until Christmas.

If increases were staggered through the year, the total dollars budgeted for salary increases wouldn't be greater, but the incentive value would be greatly enhanced.

Considering the amount of work that goes into a company's annual raise, the idea of semiannual raises may seem impossible or outrageous. But when I think of the wasted man-hours that go into unnecessary meetings and procedures, I wonder if that time might not be better spent trying to bring the raise closer to the performance.

One company already using the multiple raise as an incentive is Sisters Restaurants, based in Columbus, Ohio, which recently advertised for help and covered most of the bases as follows:

NOW HIRING

Sisters is looking for a special kind of person to work in our restaurants. We want to interview people who are willing to be trained in the newest, most exciting,

140

and fastest growing restaurant chain in Columbus.
We offer the following:

- Good hourly pay based on experience.
- *Raise and performance reviews every three months* [my italics].
- Meals—at half price.
- Employee of the Month recognition awards.
- A positive, friendly, and enthusiastic work environment.
- Flexible work schedules.
- Opportunities for career advancement through our crew leader and management trainee programs.
- Excellent training designed specifically for Sisters restaurant operations.

We provide you with more than just valuable restaurant experience. We also train you to understand standards of operations, dealing with production, quality controls, customer service, and cost controls. *We teach you important business ethics, and also show you how to develop your own personal work ethic and work skills* [my italics].
Apply in person.

I think their whole approach is terrific, but I was especially pleased to see the quarterly performance reviews and the raises that could follow.

Before I get off this subject, raises, especially merit increases, should lift the spirits of the employee and you should make the most of them. Management gets an opportunity to say "thank you" in black and white. Every raise should be accompanied by a letter from the recipient's manager or someone higher up—something that can be shown off by the employee to his spouse or family—and shared as a visible acknowledgment of work well done. I know of cases where absolutely nothing at all was made of a raise. It was added to the recipient's paycheck without a word from anyone. That's foolish. It demeans its worth. It gives the employee the feeling that the increase was either given grudgingly or pumped out by a computer and no one knows about it. *You should never miss any legitimate opportunity to add to an employee's pride and self-confidence.* If there's ever a time that calls for it, it's when you're putting money in his or her pocket.

FRINGE BENEFITS

These are an important part of the pay package, but are only marginally useful in influencing an employee's productivity. The problem is that like wages, the benefits are a given that is connected only peripherally to a person's performance. That is, retirement plans, profit sharing, and insurance programs are based on income, so the higher an employee climbs on the corporate ladder, the greater the benefits will be. Let's face it, it's tough to influence the behavior of a twenty-five-year-old by dangling a carrot that won't be fully vested for thirty or forty years. Even when a person reaches an age where a pension becomes important, the motivation is merely to survive long enough to reap the rewards of stamina and age, not to become a superb performer.

There are millions of workers who are completely satisfied with a salary-plus-benefits compensation package that is negotiated for them. They feel safe and protected. The only time they experience any pressure to compete or show off is when a higher position opens up and they might be a candidate for promotion. That doesn't mean they're happy or fulfilled, only that they are satisfied to float undisturbed on relatively quiet waters.

The company's structure, more often than not, becomes paternalistic and, in many ways, its environment takes on the qualities and troubles of a typical American family. It may be torn with personality conflicts, strained relationships, bad manners, and disrespect, but it's committed (by contract or ignorance) to protect its family members no matter what.

COMMISSIONS AND OTHER CASH INCENTIVES

The salary-plus-benefits package generally reflects the progress an employee has made with a company—the level of his responsibility, the status he's attained, his knowledge, experience, and longevity: in other words, his long-term contribution. But commissions and other cash incentives should tell a different story, focusing on another aspect of his value to the company. These are moneys paid to an employee for specific achievements and accomplishments. Usually they reflect the most *recent* impact an employee has made on the company's bottom line. To me, they're the most potent dollar incentives available to a company and its management. They draw an employee into the business, giving him a proprietary interest in the project or product being promoted. They make him a partner, not in a rhetorical sense but in reality. They tell the employee up front, "The more you produce, the more you'll make. The other side of that, of course, is the less you produce, the less you make."

The purest form of cash incentive is *straight commission* or *piecework*. The person who agrees to this type of arrangement is usually an independent agent or a freelancer. He's not considered part of the company's head count and doesn't share in any of its benefits. Since he gets paid only for what he sells

143

or produces, he can't be expected to do anything that doesn't directly impact his production. These people are entre-preneurs, sometimes independent business agents, even though, at any given time, they may be associated with a single company. In order to forgo a company's benefits, they have to earn enough in commissions to pay for their own travel and entertainment expenses, insurance, vacations, and retirement programs.

There are plenty of risks in a straight commission deal. Contracts can be broken with fairly short notice by either party. The downside for the rep is that he's totally dependent on the company's delivering the goods he's sold and keeping the promises he makes. He usually doesn't get paid until the order is shipped, sometimes until it's paid for by the customer. Unlike the company rep, who gets a paycheck no matter what happens to the order he submits, the independent may wait for months to get his commission and sometimes not get it at all.

The downside for a company having free agents selling or making its products is loss of control. A company can't expect an independent rep to spend much of his time preparing call reports, gathering customer information, or conducting sur-veys: things it routinely requests of a salaried salesperson. There's often a concern that customers may develop a greater loyalty to the agent than to the company; business would be lost if the agent takes on a competitive line.

GUARANTEED SALARY PLUS COMMISSION

For many companies, this turns out to be the best solution in selling their products. The company takes the risk away from the salesperson, guaranteeing him a salary plus expenses plus

144

the security of its benefits; in return, it "buys" the right to manage his business and oversee his performance. For thousands of reps and companies, it's a happy compromise.

I believe that the more a salesperson depends on his commissions, the more motivated he is to consistently produce. That's especially true when the rep is in a territory away from the office and his supervisor. It's a lot easier for a salesperson to stay home on a blizzardy February morning when he knows that the loss of a day's work won't affect his income that week.

When I was vice-president of IBM's worldwide marketing operations, we expected half a rep's income to be earned from sales commissions. Compared to how most companies operate, fifty percent is high, but we were committed to relate compensation as closely as possible to performance. That formula helped make us one of the best sales organizations in any industry.

Some companies set up salary-plus-commission arrangements that backfire so far as motivation is concerned. I analyzed a company that compensated its reps as follows: Each rep had to attain an annual sales quota of ninety percent of his previous year's sales before he received any commissions. Unfortunately, the salesperson who had an exceptionally good year had very little chance of scoring big two years in a row. The new quota would be jacked up so high that just meeting it would be a real accomplishment, but not enough to fatten his pocketbook. The system actually encouraged the year's high fliers to slow down and even hold back sales whenever they could. They figured that they couldn't make enough commissions, so they would do everything they could to come in with the lowest possible quota the next year. A salesperson told me that every other year, he worked his tail off trying to turn every prospect into a customer and seeing to it that every customer carried the maximum inventory of his products. In

145

fact, he made sure that they were overinventoried at the year's end. It wasn't a serious problem, he figured, because any unsold goods could be returned for full credit, so long as the return was authorized by the salesperson. The following year, when he had little chance to make a fair commission, he worked as hard to keep sales down and authorized as many returns as possible. I've heard of salespeople making unwise and unnecessary returns just to lower their next quota, then reshipping the same items after the new quota was in place—getting credit for them as new sales. Doesn't make much sense, does it? Not for the company, it doesn't.

There are companies that put in many man-hours developing equations to compute territorial commissions that will assure each salesperson a fair share of the incentive pie, but when they get done, the system cuts everyone about the same-size piece, the best performer and the worst. The so-called incentive commission becomes a given that might as well be paid out in salary. When the affected employees learn that there's little difference in compensation between the real producers and those who slide by, guess what happens to productivity and motivation.

Incentives must make sense if they are going to motivate anyone to put out extra effort. They have to reward those who do more, and not reward those who do less. As obvious as that sounds, it doesn't always happen that way. Many incentive plans in place today should be thrown out as defective. I can't imagine leading a sales force that doesn't earn a substantial part of its income by commissions.

When the commission portion of the reps' income is small —say ten percent—it's usually paid annually and isn't much of a consideration in their daily activities. In the case of IBM, where half of the reps' pay package can come from incentives, commissions are paid monthly, and you can bet they are a constant consideration in reps' daily operation.

Incentive money should be paid as close to the time it's earned as possible. The longer the employee has to wait for it, the less he can connect it to his performance.

It's easier to develop effective incentive packages for salespeople and others whose productivity can be measured regularly against a short-term expectation, than for those whose performance is more difficult to evaluate on a day-to-day basis. Whenever you can attach an incentive to an employee's performance, the more apt he is to increase his productivity and the overall level of his performance.

BONUSES

Bonuses come in all sorts of shapes and forms: money, vacations, gifts, tokens—two tickets to the theater or a check for thousands of dollars. In some cases, the rules for capturing a bonus prize are very specific, and those who are vying for them can monitor their progress much as a person who's on commission can count his incremental earnings as they accumulate. But the rules for collecting many bonuses are not well-defined and are sometimes impossible to track. Unlike commissions, bonuses can be very subjective. If they're tied to the profit of the company or a division, they may not take shape until the end of the fiscal year.

Many bonuses come in the form of a gift, and the individual may not know what factors determine how the bonus pot is divided. The gift (which I'll cover in a few minutes) can be a very exciting and dramatic way of doling out bonus money. Gifts are strong motivational incentives when they're prizes an

147

employee can shoot for—and in order to do that, he must know the rules of the game.

1. The salary-connected bonus. The most important bonus a company can pay is one connected to the employee's salary and tied directly to his performance. It should be as important to an employee who is not in sales as a commission is to a rep. This bonus must not be considered just a nice plus but an integral and necessary part of the income. Here's how it could work: An employee would receive eighty percent of the potential of his annual salary in weekly or biweekly paychecks. Every quarter, he would receive a bonus of up to twenty percent of the salary paid, depending on his performance. For example:

No bonus—minimal performance
5% bonus—fair performance
10% bonus—good performance
15% bonus—very good performance
20% bonus—excellent performance

The motivational power of this type of pay package is generated from two fronts. One, the individual believes there really is a connection between performance and earnings. Two, the manager is forced to examine the performance of the people he or she supervises.

A program like this can truly encourage and nurture what I call a meritocracy—a pay-for-performance system built on the premise that a person must be paid for what he or she produces.

2. The carrots. Whenever it's possible to give an employee a bonus to shoot for, do it! I love them, and strongly recommend the kind that incites a person to apply extraordinary efforts for a short period of time. It's exciting for an employee

148

to be challenged to produce more than is usually asked of him, especially when there are unusual exigencies. It's exhilarating to expend the extra energy and then be praised and paid for the effort when the job is completed.

3. Contests. Although I believe that competition brings excitement to the workplace, contests needn't pit employees against one another to motivate them. The most successful and welcomed contests are those in which it's possible for every participant to win and no one has to lose. These contests are usually designed to have each employee compete against his previous performance or against a criterion that's fair and equal for everyone. If the company profits by the increased productivity, why not reward everyone who contributes to that windfall? Of course, the value of the prizes must reflect the relative value of each "winner" 's contribution.

I'm against contests that have lots of people chasing after one or two prizes. I just don't see the overall motivational benefit of any program that guarantees from the start few winners.

Insurance companies are known for running contests to keep their agents out beating the bushes. Most of these contests are successful because everyone can be a winner. Each year, cruise ships and exotic vacation resorts are filled with winning agents and their spouses. The owner of a successful agency told me that these contests have a great impact on the size of the annual insurance product. On the other hand, most agents ignore the contests with two or three big winners and thousands of losers.

"Somebody wins, of course, but the 'plus sale'—what the sponsor is looking for—is puny compared to the 'plus sale' generated by the all-out, everybody-can-be-a-winner contests."

4. Bonuses that encourage creativity. There's nothing more exciting or motivating for an employee than to have his ideas taken seriously, to see them implemented, and to be rewarded when they prove profitable.

Having come out of the IBM culture, where a tremendous effort is made to draw every employee into the organizational process, I am still startled when I find companies that not only fail to draw ideas from their people but actually stifle them. To demonstrate how foolhardy it is to ignore this human resource: IBM, in the decade ending in 1985, saved *$300 million* by implementing ideas submitted by its employees. The $60 million it paid out in bonuses to those who had the ideas was a bargain for the company and a tremendous tribute to the recipients.

I don't think IBM's employees are any more creative than people in other companies, but IBM's suggestion boxes are always stuffed with ideas. The difference is in the company's attitude about drawing its people into the business. Top management knows that the employees on the line are closer to the nitty-gritty operational problems than anyone else. They're in a position to see the problems develop long before they get to the boardroom. The managers know that these people are able to recognize waste and misuse of time and materials and have ideas to improve conditions. Like any other company that truly believes its employees are a resource of intelligence and creativity, IBM actively solicits their involvement. It keeps employees aware of the importance of the suggestion box and makes a fuss over ideas that are submitted. It publishes and distributes a twenty-two-page booklet, "Your Ideas Have Value," which describes the company's various Suggestion Plans and the way to submit ideas.

I suggest that an invitation be extended by the management of every company to its employees. Tell them: We value your ideas and ask that you share them with us. We may not use all of them, but when we do, you will be rewarded.

To make the suggestion box work: *(a)* The program should be formalized, with a committee or special department set up to review and evaluate submissions. *(b)* The employees must be convinced that their ideas will be protected and they will get credit. *(c)* Every idea must be treated with respect and seriousness and everyone should receive a written reaction to his or her submissions. No one should be made to feel foolish. *The idea may or may not be important, but the person who submits it is always important.*

5. "A token of our appreciation." I've heard it said that the most difficult words a person ever has to utter are "I'm sorry." That may be, but in the business world, the two words that seem to get stuck in the throats of management most frequently are "thank you." The attitude of some management seems to be: "Our deal is, You work, I pay. 'Thank you' is not part of the agreement." That's too bad. Everybody loses.

The leadership of a company must realize that the difference between a superb performance and a mediocre one often isn't in the "deal" cut with an employee; it's in the treatment they dish out. The way management expresses its appreciation, or withholds it, either adds quality to the deal or cheapens it.

Management that doesn't make an effort to demonstrate its appreciation to employees every chance it gets is blowing some real motivational opportunities. When, in spite of such insensitive behavior, a company gets a superior performance from an employee, it probably doesn't deserve the result.

151

Expressing your appreciation in a concrete way is too important to be left to happenstance. Therefore, it makes sense to budget moneys for the purpose of saying "thank you," formally and informally, especially to employees who aren't paid commissions or eligible for other ongoing incentive plans.

I don't mean you should give bonuses or gifts to a person who's doing what's expected of him and little more, but you should look for exceptional performance and reward it. A couple of tickets to the theater or a dinner for two lets everyone in a department know that you appreciate the people who are willing to give that extra effort.

Companies wring their hands over excessive absenteeism, but not many reward those people who show up to work every day. Some companies—Mary Kay Cosmetics, for example—give bonuses each year to employees who have hundred-percent attendance records.

You may think: Come on, that's kid stuff, like the gold star they used to paste on our grade cards for perfect attendance.

But think about it; attendance awards send out several important messages to the employees: *(a)* Management knows who comes to work every day and appreciates them. *(b)* Management is very much aware of those who are absent. *(c)* Supervisors are being told, "It's your responsibility to let your people know the importance of full attendance."

Once you accept the idea that rewarding people for special feats helps lift the level of a company's performance, you view what's going on around you from a very positive vantage point. Focusing on valuable employees and exceptional performances will not only lift your own spirits, but help you solve the problems of inadequate, inefficient, and misguided performances. Just as I believe you can learn more from successes than you can from failures, I am convinced it is absolutely necessary to learn from, understand, and appreciate the best employees. Any program you can devise that will help these people surface, give them a chance to show off and be noticed, is important to them and to you.

9

All Incentives
Can't Be Banked

Any management that believes the *only* way to get a top performance out of an employee is to have him chase after a bundle of dollar bills is making a serious error. It's also a mistake for a company to believe that if you want a really top performer, all you have to do is raid a competitor. How many employers are disappointed and confused because the top dollar they paid to hire a "star" doesn't buy them the superior performance they expected? They don't understand that money alone doesn't assure consistent high-level performance.

Here's a story I recently heard that's a good example of what I'm talking about. A young professor left academia to become an account executive in a small but well-respected advertising agency. From the start, the agency was delighted with him. He was exactly what the company needed. He was talented, had abounding energy, an insatiable appetite for work, and striking leadership qualities. In short order (less than five years), he was the head of the company, and it prospered under his directorship. Anyone who watched the growth of the company had to be impressed with the positive effect he had on it. *What wasn't obvious was the positive effect the company had on him.* They provided the ideal conditions in which to perform. They gave him creative carte

157

blanche, but kept fairly tight controls over his budget. That was perfect as far as he was concerned, since there was more artist than economist in his makeup, and the arena he was working in was stimulating but safe. He fed on their enthusiasm and appreciation and responded by delivering a consistently superlative performance.

It was inevitable that a much larger company would offer him an irresistible employment contract. The money, the stock deal, and the perks were more than he had ever dreamed of attaining. But he soon found that he could not perform for his new company the way he had for the other. The chemistry wasn't the same; the dynamics were different. There was less interest and attention paid to his creative talents and tremendous concern over his ability to make big bucks. He worked in an environment that was soon festering with suspicion, jealousy, and resentment. He was challenged, all right, but it was more like a chide. "We're paying you a ton of money, so dammit, produce!" He couldn't.

The company was openly disappointed. They had made a bad investment. They probably thought the guy was burned out before he joined them or that he had been given more credit for his previous employer's success than he deserved. It's doubtful the company took any responsibility for his failure. After all, they paid him plenty, didn't they? So what happened to our young executive? After a nervous breakdown, he's now with a people-caring organization, trying to repeat his first success.

Of course, money's important. An employee who feels he's grossly underpaid won't be a good producer for long. But when we're talking about incentives that make a person stretch, it's never just the money. In fact, sometimes it's not the money at all that drives a person to achieve.

"I'M NOT IN THIS JUST FOR THE
MONEY, HONESTLY"

People don't all spend their lives chasing dollars, nor do they put a price tag on everything they do. Even the most cynical must agree with this; just consider the many educators, nurses, and artists who shrug off the so-called creature comforts because of their commitments. We can applaud these people who are driven by talent, conscience, or heritage, but their payoff comes in the experience, the accomplishment, the doing.

The cynics might disagree, but there are many people working in big corporations and small businesses who, regardless of what they're paid, approach their workday with the same excitement and intensity as the educator or the artist. It's their nature. They work in a world where the bottom line is expressed only in dollars and they know there's no pot of gold at the end of their own rainbow. What makes them run? Why are they as committed to making things work as the chairman of the board or the company's proprietor, who often reaps the financial rewards of their achievements? It's the nature of some people to do the very best they can no matter what the circumstances or what they might personally gain from their efforts. I put myself in that classification. Even though I've done well financially, money has never been the driving force behind my career. I don't think I ever asked for a raise, complained about the size of a bonus, or actively pursued a specific promotion. I went to work every morning with the idea that I would do everything possible to have a truly productive, satisfying, and exciting day. Sounds too simple, or even a cliché, but it's nevertheless true. More than anything, I needed a challenge: a problem to solve. If one wasn't waiting for me when I got to work, I'd find or create one. Of course,

I had to make a living. My first child was born while I was still an IBM trainee, and I took my personal responsibilities seriously. I was naive but at the same time right when I believed that if I did the best job I could do every single day, I'd be able to provide for my family. My personal story would be more dramatic if I worked for a company that exploited my desire to excel to my disadvantage. Fortunately, I got into a company where there was no lack of challenges and where competitive spirits were sought out, welcomed, nurtured, and rewarded. Here are some incentives that are more important than money and must be taken seriously by any company's leadership if they have any hopes of raising the energy level and productivity of its employees.

JOB SATISFACTION

Probably the greatest prize a person can get from his or her employment is job satisfaction. The best companies to work for (and these are usually the best-run companies) recognize and deal with this very important work incentive. Most companies don't. It's not that they don't care about the people who work for them; they just don't connect their employees' intuitive needs to the job at hand, and they should.

1. **People work better when they believe they're doing something important.** That's obvious, isn't it? There are no unimportant jobs in a company, and every employee should know it. It's not enough that they simply be told what they're doing is important; it's meaningless unless they understand what that means: how their job fits into the overall scheme of things and how the quality of their performance affects the overall performance of the firm. I was introduced to a young woman who worked for a firm I did business with. She seemed

embarrassed when I asked what she did there. "I'm just a clerk in Customer Service . . . take phone orders mostly."

Why should this woman feel that she is "just a clerk"? She has an important job and there is no reason for her to be apologetic about it. People who answer a business telephone have a tremendous responsibility. Once they pick up the receiver, they become the voice of the company. How they sound, the care and interest they project, and how efficiently they handle the transaction make a greater impression on the caller than the company's advertising campaign or its high-priced TV spokesperson. To anyone seeking information, this woman is more important than the company's CEO or chairman of the board, and she should know it.

Everyone's important. Each employee is in a position to add to the quality of the company's performance or detract from it. If workers don't think they make a difference and consider their work inconsequential and menial, they cannot experience job satisfaction or be consistently high achievers. For any bright manager, they are a motivational challenge.

2. People work better when they can show off their talent, education, and skills. It's often a matter of casting (like casting a show): matching the person and the task. In the long run, the toughest staffing problem for a manager occurs when an over-qualified person fills a position. It doesn't take long for the problem to surface when an underqualified employee hasn't the ability to get the job done. The manager then has options: extending the employee's training, demoting him, or severing him. It's when the employee can consistently get the job done without really applying himself and without drawing on his innate and acquired knowledge and skills that the company and the employee can eventually lose out. If an employee is put in a position where he can't flex his intellectual and creative "muscles," he'll lose interest in the job in time. If he

161

doesn't quit, he'll either get intellectually flabby or find his satisfaction outside the workplace. Even the quality of the work he does with little effort suffers because of lack of stimulation. It's a stupid and unfair situation, which can be corrected only by a sensitive management that recognizes the motivational importance of job satisfaction.

3. **The best producers respond to reasonable challenges.** My management at IBM knew from the beginning that this was the only button they had to push to get me off and running. I never had the reputation of being a creative genius or a pondering intellectual, but in time everyone in the company knew that if we had to get from here to there and had no map, I'd find a way. I love a challenge, whether it's finding a new way to distribute a computer product, reorganizing a division, or raising three children. I'm not unusual, and most of the people I've ever worked with have responded favorably to almost any challenge their companies presented.

If you're going to be an effective motivator, you must understand that employees need to feel challenged but not threatened or intimidated.

RECOGNITION

Although a person may have made the perfect connection of his interests and skills to an occupation, his morale, loyalty, and level of ambition will be determined largely by the recognition he receives in and out of the company. There are many ways an employee can be given appropriate recognition, and I don't think any of the possibilities should be shrugged off as unnecessary or superficial. They all add to the person's pride and esteem.

162

1. **Promotions.** Although money usually accompanies a promotion, there are greater motivational aspects than just the fatter paycheck. (A bit of trivia just crossed my mind: When I was in the army, the difference between a buck private's and a sergeant's pay was less than a dollar a day: hardly an incentive to struggle for the stripes!) A promotion usually connotes added responsibility, authority, and power, and is certainly a signal to co-workers, family, and friends that the recipient is being recognized and rewarded by an appreciative management.

2. **New title, same job.** Sometimes it's important to promote a person even though there's no real change in his duties or responsibilities. A problem occurs when an employee's in a job where there's little opportunity or desire for him to climb the corporate ladder. For example, in many companies a great salesperson can have the title Marketing Representative for twenty or thirty years. The company would be foolish to pull him out of a successful territory and bring him into the home office to fill a position for which he has no experience or real interest. Besides, they probably couldn't afford to match his present income. If he was pressured to take a managerial position and relocate his family, the promotion would be anything but motivational. It would be a punishment. The solution is to have levels, with titles that reflect the expertise, professionalism, and wisdom that come with years of problem-solving experiences and solid sales successes. I'm not impressed with titles such as Sales Engineer because it seems as if you're giving the salesperson a college degree he or she never earned. A sales rep could become a senior marketing rep, a master account rep, or an account executive. The point is that it's important to award your top performers titles that carry status and

163

can be shown off with pride: if not by them, then by their husband or wife.

3. Other status symbols. Ever since the days of Vance Packard, many people won't admit to being motivated by badges of success, but most are. It's especially true of those who yearn for a sign that their good work is not going unnoticed, and hope to separate themselves from their peers.

In the corporate world, an employee's *working space* is often a symbol of his achievement and a performance incentive. Moving from one of several desks in an open area to an office with a door is like relocating from an inner-city slum to the suburbs. I've seen people become ecstatic when they were given an office with windows and a view, and others who became hysterical because they lost a window or were stuck with the "house carpet." Top management sets the standards for these status symbols and makes them an issue when office size, location, and trappings are determined by title and rank, not need. I don't like to see a caste system develop in a company. To me, there's no logical reason for executive dining rooms, exclusive johns, or reserved parking spaces. Incentives and rewards that are available to relatively few can be demoralizers and demotivators for the rest.

What I have to say about *company cars,* especially those furnished to a field sales force, may seem like a contradiction to my thoughts about office space, but bear with me. As I mentioned before, most marketing people never move into managerial ranks, but not because they aren't good at their jobs. For them, prestige comes as their professionalism matures, but usually they don't have an office or a staff or any of the artifacts that spell success. Since most salespeople spend as much time in their company cars as their managers do in their offices, the automobile should be used as a motivational factor and a symbol of a company's appreciation. The salesperson

164

who's been a profitable producer for fifteen or twenty years and continues to produce deserves more than the stripped-down automobile that's easily spotted as a company car. I'd like the most productive or honored salespeople to drive in style. Cars mean something. It would give successful reps and their families a lift to park more than just a low-cost automobile in their driveway.

THE PROMISE OF SECURITY

I must admit to having a problem with this. Although some people put security high on their list of reasons for working at a job, I don't see it as a major motivator for a high-level performance. I don't believe in tenure. For thirty-four years, every day of my business life, I listened for those footsteps, and some days they were louder than others. Sure, you respect what someone has done in the past, but you have to produce on a current basis. The problem is that no company can afford to carry nonproductive people, regardless of whether they've been with them one year or ten years. That's why it's so important to weed out the nonproductive employees, not only in their first year but on a continuing basis.

I do understand how an employee working in an unstable, insecure environment may have trouble staying "up," excited, and ambitious. It's terrible when the jobs of hard-working, productive people are put in jeopardy every time there's a downturn in business. There's no doubt in my mind that companies that strive to maintain a full-employment practice have the best chance of keeping a high motivation level among their people. Again, I don't think it's guaranteed security that's an incentive. Real motivation comes with the employees' belief that their performance, not a contract, will protect their future.

165

APPRECIATE THE EXTRA EFFORT

Thank you. Thank you. Thank you. These words are always on the tip of the best leaders' tongue. They know people respond positively to appreciation, compliments, and recognition, even when they protest that they work just as hard without positive reinforcement. We all know how the attention moves us. When it comes to others, most of us seem to file the notion away as though it were inconsequential trivia. Successful leaders don't.

Years ago, when I was a teen, a popular syndicated newspaper columnist named Dr. George Crane solicited membership to what he called "The Three-Compliments-a-Day Club." He believed that if you joined, (1) you'd be motivated to look for the good around you, (2) you would make at least three people happy, (3) you'd feel good about yourself, and (4) people would be drawn to you. The idea of a compliment club seems pretty corny today. Maybe it did forty or fifty years ago, when Crane dreamed it up, but giving recognition was wanting then and it still is. Believe me, the top motivators have always understood the need.

If you want a positive response to your suggestions and demands, remember the following:

1. Get out of your office. When someone does something exceptionally good for the company, pay him or her a visit and express your appreciation. Think of how much more the praise means if you go to the employee's office instead of calling him to yours. It enhances the compliment.

2. Don't keep good works secret. Make sure that your management knows about the exceptional efforts of the employees you manage, and ask them to recognize their accomplishments. I wanted the managers and people under me to let me know when someone did something special for the company or a customer and I always sent a handwritten note of appreciation to let them know that their achievements did not go unnoticed. It's frustrating and worrisome for an employee when his special efforts receive no recognition. He may feel they were wasted efforts as far as his management is concerned. Even worse, he may feel that his boss is taking credit for his work, and no one knows what he's doing.

3. Thank people publicly. Exceptional performances should be publicized whenever possible: in house organs and memos, at meetings and conferences.

Formalize the appreciation whenever it's appropriate. I like it when I walk into a business place and see a plaque on the wall announcing the "Employee of the Month." I know the company is actively looking for ways to motivate its people by seeking out superior performers and giving them proper recognition.

If you think your employees are too sophisticated or professional to respond to recognition awards, you're probably wrong. Don't your Ph.D.s still advertise their doctorates even when they've been out of school for twenty years and have no direct connection with academia? How many people still wear college class rings, fraternity or sorority pins, or other badges of recognition?

People like to belong to exclusive clubs whether they admit it or not: the Million Dollar Round Table, the President's Club, the 100 Percent Club (100 percent of quota, sales, attendance, etc.); they work for the recognition and the benefits. I remember sitting on a veranda in Hawaii, listening to a conversation between an IBM marketing rep and his wife. This was the first year he'd achieved membership in the company's Golden Circle. To attain that honor and be eligible to attend the group's annual convention, he had to rank in the top ten percent of the sales organization. The words that grabbed my attention were uttered by the employee's spouse: "You better bring me back here next year!" She was happy and laughing. She was also helping management motivate her spouse to aspire for continued success and high-level achievements.

If your company hasn't embraced incentives like these, take it upon yourself to encourage them.

CONTINUING EDUCATION, AN IMPORTANT MOTIVATOR

You want your people to be excited about life. Minds that are curious and analytical should be nurtured by intellectual stimulation. Motivated people boost the productivity of everyone around them. Encourage your employees to take as many courses as they can. A course needn't be directly related to their work so long as it lifts their spirits and keeps them intellectually alive. The employee who's willing to put in the time should be given special recognition for completing any course successfully. The cost is a wise investment for a company.

Ongoing in-house training programs are absolutely necessary to give employees the confidence and tools to strive for more responsibility and higher achievements. Successful companies recognize the great importance of continuing education and treat the cost as a vital investment, not as an expense to be used sparingly. IBM, for example, provides forty hours of education for every employee, regardless of his or her position or length of employment. Milliken, a leading textile company, does the same thing.

Not only do top companies invest in their employees' continuing education; they provide time for "civic dues." For example, IBM grants employees time off to teach in black universities and encourages others to use their expertise for the community good. It's hard to measure the payoff for the company, but all these things elevate the stature of the employee, and have positive motivational influence on his job performance.

A POTENT MOTIVATOR

There are countless ways to motivate others without putting money in their purses. One of the most reliable and effective is by demonstrating your enthusiasm for them. Your approval, respect, faith, confidence, loyalty, and support are all part of it. How you show your interest to the people who look to you for leadership and guidance depends on your own personality and management style. To me, the greatest motivators are those who are straightforward. They never play psychological warfare or any head games with their people. They have the ability to express their interest and still maintain businesslike relationships by understanding that these people need leadership more than they need friendship. On the other hand, neither do the best motivators try to solicit affection, or take a proprietary interest in the people they want to inspire and develop.

Motivate your people by fighting the system for bonuses, raises, and promotions when they're deserved. Demonstrate your sincere interest by holding them back when they're not ready for new responsibilities. Praise them in public, but criticize them in private. Be fair and respectful.

Never underestimate the importance of your enthusiasm,

169

not only for your employees but for your job, your products and services, and your company.

Finally, remember this: *If you want the people who work for you to strive for their best possible performance, then give them as much responsibility as they can handle. Give them room to breathe and develop, and hold them accountable for what they do.*

10

The Company's Hidden Challenge: The Drug and Alcohol Problem

How can we get the best out of ourselves and others if we don't do something about the greatest of all demotivators —the drug and alcohol abuse that is reaching epidemic proportions in our society?

Illegal drug use is so widespread that it permeates every business, profession, economic level, social group, and school.

IT'S A BIG, BAD, MERCILESS BUSINESS

The production, distribution, and sale of illegal drugs is one of the biggest industries in this country today—and it's growing at a rate any legitimate business would envy. It's estimated that in 1986, Americans spent more than $110 billion on illegal drugs. To put that figure in perspective, the total equity of the six largest U.S. companies comes to just $116 billion.

It's almost impossible to believe that Americans consume sixty percent of the world's production of illegal drugs. We are the marketplace coveted by every criminal drug grower, processor, manufacturer, packager, distributor, and pusher. The government estimates that twenty-five percent of our population uses illegal drugs occasionally or frequently, with twenty million regular users of marijuana, eight million users of cocaine, and well over five hundred thousand users of heroin.

The drug problem is not a throwback to the '60s, nor is it particular to any one socioeconomic group. No school superintendent, principal, or teacher can tell you his or her school has no drug problem. By their mid-twenties, eighty percent of all Americans—some of them kids as young as eight years old—have tried illegal drugs. If anyone believes the drug problem is a ghetto problem and the users are minority kids, then they are out of touch with reality. Seventy-five percent of today's young users are from affluent communities.

David Toma, the ex–narcotics detective from New Jersey who has devoted the past twenty years to fighting drugs in the schools, says: "I've been in every kind of school in the U.S.—elementary, junior and senior high—I've spoken to kids in fancy private schools (boys and girls), military academies, parochial schools, and public schools—inner-city, suburban, and rural—and I find the same thing. They're all illegal drugstores and supermarkets. Kids can get hold of almost anything they want to get high—a joint, a snort, a vial, a pill, or a drink. They want to get high, more and more of them every day, and every year the customers get younger."

To quote from a 1986 article in *Think* magazine, written by Patricia Brooks, "Depressing as all the statistics and revelations are, Americans are beginning to fight back. Too many families have now been touched by the pestilence of drugs, and there are positive signs that grass roots organizations are being formed to combat the epidemic. An even more hopeful sign is that businesses are beginning to take a tough stand against drug abuse."

BUSINESS HAS TO BECOME
INVOLVED

Since the President and Nancy Reagan took a strong anti-drug position, there has been greater resolve on our government's part to fight the illegal drug industry; but much of its effort has done little more than provide expensive aggravation to the professional drug dealer. So long as there is an ever-growing market, drug entrepreneurs will find a way to supply that demand. Our law enforcement people may be lamenting the fact that there's no way to seal off our thousands of miles of coastline and borders from the dope smugglers; but business and industry can and must do something to protect themselves, and they must do it now.

I'm convinced that the drug problem is present in every business and industry in every state of this country. Two thirds of the people entering the work force today have tried illegal drugs. The leadership of any firm that, for any reason, denies the drug problem or chooses to ignore it is either foolish, weak, misguided, or dangerously naive. We in business must put the drug problem high on our list of priorities. It's a matter of self-preservation. It's also a matter of protecting company employees and customers.

THE INCREMENTAL COSTS

A continuous flow of studies present undeniable evidence of the shocking costs of drugs and alcohol in the workplace. In addition to the $110 billion that's sapped from the economy each year, drug and alcohol abuse on the job has caused a $110 billion decline in productivity in America. This includes the costs of drug- and alcohol-induced accidents, absenteeism,

175

mechanical foul-ups, and white-collar crime directly related to this insidious problem.

Right now we are able to put a price tag of over $200 billion on illegal drug use, but the greatest costs cannot be quantified. Partly, its the price we pay for the mental errors, faulty judgments, and mismanagement resulting from drug use and alcoholism. What's even more alarming is the potential long-range damage not only to business and industry but to all our institutions. I'm talking about the way drug and alcohol abuse affects the general level of total performance—what it does to ambition, how it suppresses motivation, and its effect on a person's ability to reason.

American business, like American society, has been hurt badly. Drugs are changing the quality and potential of our most important resource—the human resource. Unless we do something about it, the damage will be irreversible.

Anyone who thinks my attitude is an overreaction, unfair, or immoral doesn't understand the depth and seriousness of the drug epidemic. We tend to ignore such a problem until it explodes in our faces. The drug problem, which took root in the early 1900s, spans every segment of our society. Since the 1960s, a significant percentage of our children have experimented with drugs to some extent—and millions of them grow up and make drugs like marijuana a part of their lifestyle and culture. Where are these people now, the ones who get high on a regular basis? You see the most unfortunate, the ones who kept experimenting with drugs, living in the streets and abandoned buildings of our cities, scrounging for drug money—begging, mugging, killing for it. You read about those who became drug entrepreneurs, spreading the poison into every part of society. Many are in the workplace, lowering our standards, increasing our costs, damaging the environment around them. They are in every business, institution, and profession. Some work in our hospitals and nursing homes; some assemble our cars, fly our airplanes, and work at every level in every type of business. They use our equipment, negotiate our contracts, and handle our money. I don't like it. I don't think anyone who strives for excellence can tolerate such a situation.

THE COMPANY'S DIRECT APPROACH

I think every company has the responsibility and the right to take a hard-line, self-protective, paternalistic position to get drugs out of its organization; and the most direct route is to close the door on the drug user.

First, we must approach the problem with the attitude that drug users are victims of a contagious, unlawful subculture. We in business must declare that there is no place in the work force for people who use illegal drugs. I know that such a statement sounds harsh and unfeeling, but it isn't. Every company has to do what it can to educate employees about drugs and help rehabilitate people who are drug-dependent. We must be careful not to further victimize these people, but the drug problem should be attacked at every level.

The U.S. Department of Health and Human Services (NIAAA, NIDA) estimates that: drug- and alcohol-impaired employees are 28 percent less productive than nonusers; their absenteeism runs two to four times the national average; they're involved in three to four times as many accidents as nonusers; and their rates of satisfactory job performance and poor decisionmaking are three to four times those of nonusers. Isn't it the company's responsibility to reduce the risks however it can?

It's a company's obligation to protect the interests of its investors, its customers, and all its employees. How can a business afford to handicap itself with high-risk drug- and alcohol-

177

dependent employees who erode quality, reduce efficiency, drive up costs and prices, and endanger the lives of others?

A company has the right and the responsibility to make sure that the people who are being promoted into supervisory, management, and decisionmaking positions aren't going to subtly lower the company's standards because of chemicals that impair their judgmental abilities.

A company has the right and the responsibility to keep criminals out of its work force. Wait a minute before you start climbing all over me. Most in-house crimes are drug-related. At twenty-five dollars a dose, a cocaine user can quickly build a habit that robs him of most or all of his legitimate income. He may try to pay for his habit by becoming a dealer or else resort to theft and fraud. Drug users even become entrepreneurs, selling the company's products and equipment "out the back door." Sometimes their business is joined by the tough professional criminal who gets access to the company's facilities and assets.

THE MAJOR ROLE OF
BUSINESS IN THE SOLUTION

Every business has to convince its employees that drugs are the enemy; that an employee's continued use of drugs will cost him dearly *today* and will surely devastate his future.

Recreational users do not believe there is a negative trade-off for them, and that's a problem. One, they don't believe that drugs can be addictive—at least, for them. Sadly, the drug-dependent person still thinks he's in charge of his life, long after he's lost control. Two, users are not worried about the law or its enforcement. The odds against being arrested, indicted, and convicted of a drug charge for possession or use are so small as to seem irrelevant. Three, people don't realize the effect drugs have on their performance, so they don't consider it a problem in the workplace. Chances are, their employers have never demonstrated concern about drugs, so the attitude is: What the heck is there to worry about?

Well, business may not be able to convince users that drugs are addictive and dangerous or to become part of the law enforcement complex; but it certainly can have an effect on the attitudes expressed in number three above.

Drug users and alcohol abusers will begin to take notice when business and industry openly declare war on drugs and resolve to rid their ranks of this madness. The users will take notice when business and industry treat illegal drug use as the crime it is and take action against those who sell or distribute illegal drugs in the workplace. Business will make a difference with this message to the user: Give up drugs and seek help, or give up your job!

Agreeing with this is easy; implementing it is not. However, I implore all businesses to take the difficult but unshakable position to become drug-free. This means putting in place two things: a drug-testing program; and an established and clearly articulated drug policy.

THE VERY HARD COMMITMENTS

1. Refuse to employ anyone who is alcohol or drug dependent or uses drugs recreationally. This has to become policy—and part of your recruiting and hiring practices. Every applicant must know from the outset that he or she must be drug-free to be seriously considered for a position.

What I suggest here may call for affidavits or declarations signed by applicants, and testing. Every employee should expect to be fired if his or her use of drugs affects the workplace. Employment agencies, headhunters, and campus recruiters should know your policy. Whenever you advertise for employees—regardless of the level or position—you should state your anti-drug position.

Please do not discriminate against ex-users. These people have been victimized enough. If they've been able to overcome their addiction or drug dependence, they deserve a second chance.

2. Employees should be drug tested before they're promoted into a management job or an equivalent position. All employees must be free of drugs if they expect to have a healthy and profitable career with a company. The message that must be given over and over again is: "Drug use is not acceptable and will not be tolerated by the company. You may have to choose between your career with us and drugs."

3. Reserve the right to test current employees for drugs and alcohol when there is probable cause, and make such testing part of an ongoing program. This is tougher to do than screening applicants, because you know the people, and they mean a great deal to you. It mustn't matter, though, because drug sickness is a creeping disease; it nibbles away at a company's vitality and does its damage before the symptoms are understood or the problem is diagnosed. Besides, the sickness is contagious. Most newcomers to drug use are indoctrinated by either friends, colleagues, or co-workers. *Each employee should expect to be tested for drugs if management determines that he or she has a drug problem.* Anyone who refuses to be tested should be suspended without pay until he or she complies or is severed.

4. Any valued employee who fails the test should be given the opportunity to rid himself of the chemical substances and retested after a proper interval.

5. The company should underwrite the cost of a drug or alcohol rehabilitation program for permanent employees who have become drug dependent or addicted. An employee who refuses a rehab program should be severed.

6. After the company's position is publicized, anyone discovered with illegal drugs when working for the company—on or off the premises—should be fired at once. Employees should be given adequate notice that you will not tolerate the presence of any illegal chemical substances in your company's facilities or on an employee's person.

The above commitments are not easy or pleasant to implement; however, they will help increase a company's productivity, enhance its profits, and improve its general state of well-being. The alternative—doing little or nothing about drugs in the workplace—will eventually sap most of a company's creativity and vitality.

MANY NONUSERS WILL OBJECT TO THESE TESTS

When you consider the fact that two thirds of the people entering the work force have tried illegal drugs—and the fact that drug and alcohol abuse on the job costs businesses $110 billion a year—is it any wonder that thirty percent of the *Fortune* 500 companies have instituted some form of drug screening for applicants and/or employees?

Drug users will not be the only ones who balk at being tested. Some nonusers will object as a matter of principle or to protect friends. The objectors will come from every level of the organization. Difficult as it is, the leadership of your company must take a strong stand and fend off the objections, no matter what.

181

I know about the invasion-of-privacy arguments against drug testing and the notion that such policies foster distrust between employer and employee. Popular points are made, but I don't think they should cloud or interfere with the real issue. *Drugs should be eliminated from the workplace.*

I would fight any union, employee association, or organization on this issue. To protect a person's right to use illegal drugs is ludicrous. To hinder a company's attempt to rid itself of drugs is outrageous. Possession and use of illegal drugs are punishable crimes. Users have no moral recourse.

Any company that employs more than a handful of people had better consider whether there are drug users on its payroll and maybe even illegal drugs on its premises.

Business must send out a message that it will not knowingly hire or keep on its payrolls anyone who uses illegal drugs; and it will do everything possible to screen out the users. Periodic random drug testing is now done in occupations involving security and safety: the police, subway and train operations, pilots and air traffic controllers. To quote Patricia Brooks in *Think* magazine, "Perhaps industry should adopt the watchwords used by the U.S. Navy as part of its $24 million anti-drug program, on walls and sailors' T-shirts: 'Not on my watch, not on my ship, not in my Navy.' As one Navy captain put it, 'It's a war, and the enemy is drugs.' "

IBM FACES THE DRUG PROBLEM

If any company could be smug about its employees and consider the drug problem to be something other firms have to worry about, I suppose that company is IBM. Consecutively voted one of the most respected U.S. companies in *Fortune* magazine's annual survey, IBM has a reputation of being squeaky clean. Even as careful as its employment practices are

182

and as ingrained as its culture is, IBM does not consider itself immune to the drug epidemic. After all, it employs about 400,-000 people.

IBM began drug testing job applicants at all U.S. facilities in 1985. I don't think the company ever hired anyone who tested positive. If an applicant refuses to be tested, he or she will not be considered for employment. It's important to note that the testing is so structured that if the first, presumptive test given is positive, a much more stringent test is required for confirmation.

Although the company does not now routinely test current employees, it will ask for a test if there is reason to believe an employee is using drugs. IBM's managers attend awareness programs to help them—with the assistance of a medical staff —identify employees who may have a drug problem and get those employees the rehabilitative support needed, through efforts like the Employee Assistance Program. Management isn't on a witch hunt, but it's trained to recognize probable symptoms of drug and alcohol abuse and expected to initiate some action when the circumstantial evidence warrants it. It's sensitive to what is considered "high-risk" employee behavior, such as: absenteeism, tardiness, accidents on the job, physiological symptoms, frequent unapproved breaks, job-related memory lapses, and verbal or physical abuse of co-workers.

Obviously, it takes a combination of these things to arouse one's suspicions—along with other behavioral concerns: perhaps a high frequency of phone calls and visits that are not job related, the use of code words or passwords, vague impromptu meetings, phone conversations that end abruptly.

Keep in mind that managers are not doctors, but if they sense a problem they will ask for a medical evaluation. The medical professional then determines if a drug test is an appropriate part of the overall medical situation.

Also, it's encouraging to note, individuals many times will

seek help on their own through employee assistance programs, without any management knowledge or involvement. Today, there are some five thousand employee assistance programs nationwide, with sixty percent of all *Fortune* 500 companies providing assistance for employees with drug or alcohol problems.

The responsible people in a company should know something about the behavioral effects drugs have on a person. Here's a one-minute guide:

1. Cannabis *(marijuana, hashish, hash oil).* Users experience short-term memory loss, lack of depth perception, decrease in initiative. They may snack frequently and drink lots of water. Pot has a sweet smell, which may be detected on users' bodies. You can see redness in the person's eyes, and pot use makes the eyes quite sensitive.

2. Alcohol *(liquor, beer, wine, fortified wine).* One drink can affect a person for an hour, four drinks for five hours. The drinker is often late after lunch, disappears during work hours, has a high rate of absenteeism, has accidents on and off the job, suffers a loss of job skills and coordination. His memory may become impaired, he can be subject to trembling, have pink or red eyes and an alcohol odor on his breath or about his body.

3. Stimulants *(cocaine, amphetamines).* Behavior is inconsistent; users experience lots of highs and lows, they often become hyper, appearing very busy but not being very productive. Cocaine users may sniffle a lot, have dilated eyes and a dry mouth. This drug alters the brain chemistry and damages the nerves; it causes headaches and insomnia.

4. Depressants *(Quaaludes, Valium, etc.).* Users may appear drowsy, manifest slurred speech and impaired memory.

They may appear drunk, even have the shakes, but there is no telltale smell.

5. Opiates *(heroin, opium, morphine, methadone)*. These users usually become dealers and thieves. They are accident prone and disappear from the job frequently. They may have visible tracks on their arms, "pinned" eyes, cigarette burns on their hands, and runny noses.

6. Psychedelics *(LSD, DMT, mescaline, peyote, psilocybin)*. A single dose can last up to twelve hours. The user can be easily distracted, act odd or peculiar, become fascinated with obscure objects, experience a total loss of depth perception, and at times become hysterical.

7. Inhalants *(glue, cleaning fluid, gasoline, Freon, etc.)*. Users exhibit severely impaired memory, lack of coordination, dizziness, impaired vision. They suffer unusual weight loss, running eyes and nose, and have telltale red around the nostrils.

Depending on whose statistics you read—government or private studies—anywhere from twelve to twenty percent of the U.S. work force mess around with drugs and abuse alcohol. I don't blame any company for doing whatever it can to keep such people off its employment rolls.

Again, I emphasize that what is required is a compassion for those who have become users. They must be given a chance for rehabilitation, but if unwilling to accept help, then they should be released from the business.

11

The Employees' Hidden Challenge: Waging War on Drug and Alcohol Abuse

of the company, so long as they still got paychecks. Second, although hundreds of thousands of dollars were made off the stolen goods, almost all the money ended up in the hands of the drug dealer. The others received their share in powder, pills, capsules, vials, and bags of weed. *Not only did these people pay with their health, their careers, and their freedom; they cost many innocent people their jobs too.*

NO GREATER ACT OF
SELF-DISRESPECT

Early in this book, I spoke about the need for the individual to be respected and to respect himself. Aside from suicide, I can think of no greater act of self-disrespect than taking drugs or abusing alcohol. Otherwise intelligent people, who would never play Russian roulette with a single cartridge in a six-shooter, play as deadly a game day in, day out. They ingest poisonous chemicals that are processed in unsanitary "labs" by amateur chemists and often distributed by gangsters and murderers. The drugs are peddled by pushers who might do anything from spraying the substance with roach powder to adding horse tranquilizers to the mix, or rat poison or cyanide—anything to enhance the high and satisfy the customer, until it kills him or turns him into a killer or drives him insane. Do you think I'm exaggerating? Sit in a criminal courtroom for a while. Visit a prison. Tour a mental hospital ward. You will see people who never dreamed they could be had by a pill, a snort, or a smoke.

Most of our vehicular deaths and maimings are drug and alcohol related. Most of our violent crimes are drug related. A high percentage of our white-collar crimes are drug related. Many of the emotional and mental breakdowns, especially of our young people, are drug related. *I say that no self-respecting person takes drugs today.*

Some people argue it's unfair that mind- and mood-altering drugs are illegal when tobacco and alcohol are not only legal but government regulated, subsidized in the case of tobacco and state merchandised in the case of alcohol. There are other mind-boggling contradictions: it's illegal to drive over 55 mph, but we manufacture automobiles that easily travel 85 to 100 mph; cheap handguns or "Saturday night specials" are legally manufactured yet seem to end up in the hands of criminals. None of these things make sense, but the madness of those legal aberrations in no way weakens the case against drugs anywhere in our society.

UNDERSTAND THE PROBLEM

We have to start by separating the truth about drug use from the fantasy. Well, this is the truth: *All* recreational drugs are harmful, dangerous, and costly—to the people who use them, to the people who work with users, and to the companies that hire the users. There are popular perceptions about some drugs that are totally off base. For instance, marijuana is still considered by many users to be, of all drugs, the most innocent and benign; yet it is having a damaging effect on this country's productivity, efficiency, and future development.

Smoking marijuana was widely practiced by young people in the 1960s and became an anti-establishment symbol for that generation. Kids believed the likes of Jerry Rubin and Timothy Leary. Drugs were fun and no more dangerous than tobacco. Many knew that it was illegal, but what the heck; so was beer at one time; the law simply hadn't caught up with social realities. Then there were the irresponsible messages they were receiving from people who should have known better. In the mid-'70s, the director of the National Institute on Drug Abuse issued a statement that was picked up by the national wire services. It gave the dope pushers a certain credibility and gave the kids an answer to parents who were worried about their kids taking dope. He said that marijuana "was less of a hazard to health than tobacco or alcohol."

He was wrong; his statement was based on old information. He evidently didn't know that the THC content in marijuana was fifty times greater in 1970 than it was in 1960. Or that the almost one hundred poisonous chemicals in pot compound into about four hundred different poisons when they are sucked into the lungs and transported through the bloodstream. By 1978, this director knew that he had made a terrible mistake and issued the following statement, which was quoted in the *Washington Post:*

"I get a very sick feeling in the pit of my stomach when I hear talk about marijuana being safe. Marijuana is a very powerful agent which is affecting the body in many ways. What the full range of these consequences is going to prove to be, we can only guess at this point. From what we already know, I have no doubt they are going to be horrendous."

A year later, he was quoted in *Reader's Digest,* saying that youngsters who smoke marijuana "are making guinea pigs of themselves in a tragic national experiment."

Later, he told Edwin Newman: "This is a disaster, and I feel very badly that I contributed to it."

People say, "Hey, I don't smoke pot on the job. Maybe a little to relax me in the evening or to socialize on the weekends. I'm not an addict; I use pot the same way a social drinker has a cocktail before dinner and wine with his meal. No difference, right?"

Wrong! Completely wrong. The alcohol in beer, wine, or liquor can play havoc with the way a person functions while it's in his or her bloodstream; however, alcohol is water soluble and passes through the body in a matter of hours. So the alcohol taken into your system at dinner will have been excreted before you go to work the next day. THC—the chemical substance in marijuana that produces the desired high—is more complex than alcohol. For one thing, it isn't water soluble, it's fat soluble. It doesn't pass through the body in hours or even a day: it can take from thirty or more days to be eliminated from the body and brain. A weekend pot smoker keeps building up THC in his body, and where is this poison stored? In the fatty tissue of the brain, the lungs, the reproductive system, and other organs. The regular user may not feel high when he gets to work, but the chemical in his system could affect his reaction time, his ability to process and retain information, and weaken his motivation. I don't want him working for me!

Crack, a deadly drug that's made by cooking cocaine with either baking soda or a solvent, is being marketed to the widest possible audience. That is, it's being sold in ten- and fifteen-dollar units, so a person's initiation is inexpensive. No drug has ever spread in popularity as quickly as this one. That's partly because it gives a tremendous high *instantly.* On inhalation, it reaches the brain in less than ten seconds. Its immediacy and intensity make it a delight to drug users, who are forever looking for a quicker and greater chemical "rush." What makes it work faster than ordinary cocaine is the direct route it takes to the brain, traveling with the oxygen as well as through the bloodstream. The fact that the duration of the high is only two to five minutes may be a slight disappointment to the beginning user; but it's a bonanza to the producers and distributors, and herein lies the most terrifying aspect of this new "miracle" drug: *It boasts an unbelievably high addiction rate.*

There are people who protest the evaluation of every new drug that hits the streets.

"You always overstate the risks and the damage," they say. "You try to scare us to death, and when we find out you exaggerated, you lose your credibility."

Baloney. Our problem is that we don't react quickly enough or harshly enough. How many years did it take before we had any idea how damaging a drug marijuana is?

Cocaine was virtually glamorized in the '70s as the "drug of choice" for young, upwardly mobile people. Has the danger of cocaine been overstated? How many careers have been ruined by it? How many people have turned to crime to pay for it? How many surgeries have been performed in attempts to repair the damage the drug has done to nasal passages and sinus cavities?

If crack is anywhere near as addictive as it's reported to be, it could scramble the lives of millions of people. A young crack addict, interviewed on television, said that his ten-dollar introduction to the drug quickly turned into a six-hundred-dollar-a-week habit and it's growing. That's not much for a drug habit; some spend that every day. Where do people get the money to support such habits? They push drugs for it. They steal, maim, and kill for it. They become prostitutes for it. The damage it will do in terms of crime and loss to business, industry, and our institutions is more than anyone can project. Even without crack, drugs can bring this country down unless we take our stand now.

THE INDIVIDUAL'S RESPONSIBILITY

One person can make a difference in this world. It's time for every person to stay free of drugs and to take a strong, open, vocal anti-drug position. Take the position that there's little or no difference between your friend or colleague who snorts cocaine at a fashionable suburban party and the addict who shoots up heroin in an alley in New York. There is no moral or ethical difference between the two and certainly no greater justification for the "nice" people to poison themselves and their society than for the desperate addict.

The facts about drugs are better known today. The information's out there, begging to be read and taken seriously. Say No to Drugs clubs are forming all over America; Tough Love groups offer help to families that suffer drug problems; and drug rehab centers are springing up everywhere. There's M.A.D.D. (Mothers Against Drunk Driving) and other anti-drug action groups. The American Association of Advertising Agencies has launched a massive media War on Drugs campaign. Because of the serious drugs-in-sports problems, radio and television are devoting more time to anti-drug programming than ever before and the press has given more space to the drug problem. There's plenty of documentation today. Malcolm Smith's warning of the dangers of marijuana, *With Love from Dad*, was basically a compilation of 758 scientific and medical studies. His work just scratched the surface of the body of information now available. Nobody can enter the drug scene as innocently as many did twenty years ago. Still we read that the epidemic continues to spread. It will continue to spread so long as we, individually, fail to fight it.

Any nonuser who, for whatever reason, doesn't openly declare himself hostile to drug use makes a frightening statement of acceptance and encouragement.

Leave the dinner or the party when someone brings out the pot, the powder, or the pills, and let them know why you're leaving.

Don't let the users put you on the defensive. Ingesting poison, short-circuiting the impulses in your brain, sucking a chemical into a cavity in your skull where there is no lymphatic system to protect you against infection, isn't chic or modern or bright—it's stupid. I know a guy who won't eat eggs or red meat because he worries about cholesterol, but he smokes marijuana daily. He's a nut. I know a woman who counts calories and jogs three miles a day and snorts cocaine. She's an idiot. Don't let people like these intimidate you. Let them know that their lifestyle is unacceptable to you.

If you're clean of drugs, you must discourage their use by your co-workers. It's not easy, but you must let them know that you disapprove. If they work for you, do not tolerate drug or alcohol use. Encourage counseling or rehabilitation, but let them know that they're putting their jobs in jeopardy. If the company you work for doesn't have a formal anti-drug policy, then you must strive to have one activated.

No matter what, stay clean yourself. Don't allow anyone or any situation to cause you to poison your body and impair your performance. You need all the advantages possible to compete in the marketplace of the '90s and beyond; and drugs and alcohol can quickly negate all the important skills you've developed over the years.

DON'T LET THE SIZE OF THE PROBLEM DISCOURAGE YOU

The illegal drug problem in the United States is so big and so terrible that it can easily overwhelm the individual. When we think of it as a $100,000,000,000.00 (that's $100 billion) American industry serving as many as 50,000,000 users, we may get the idea that it's too big for any individual to fight. Ideally, we should band together and rattle the rafters with our outrage. We, the nonusers, are still the majority. We've been a silent majority too long. We need to become loud and outspoken, unyielding and inflexible, angry and intolerant. We must take a firm position at home. *No drugs, no matter what.* That means parents as well as children. We must take a firm position in our schools. *No drugs, no matter what.* That means teachers, administrators, and all employees, as well as children. We must take a firm position in business and industry. *No drugs, no matter what.* That means in the boardroom and at expensive lunches, as well as on the assembly line and in the mailroom.

We will never win the battle against drugs if there is easy access to illicit drugs and acceptance of their use. What is needed is a balanced, joint effort at reducing supplies, saying no to drugs, and providing the user with an opportunity to clean up. The rehabilitation of the drug-dependent person is a personal and social gain. It's the only way.

12

"Lend Me Your Ears"

Although I began speaking to large groups when I was a class officer in high school, I never expected to become a public speaker. It never occurred to me that much of my success would depend on my ability to motivate an audience, or that after retirement from IBM, I would build a new and exciting career as a professional speaker.

Like many people in sales, managerial, and executive positions, I was frequently required to speak to groups when it was the most expedient way to sell my ideas, explain my position, or impart information. As a sales manager and, later, vice-president of marketing, I had no choice but to speak before hundreds, sometimes thousands of marketing reps and push as many motivational buttons as I could. It was my responsibility to lift their spirits, exhort them to shun mediocrity, make them want to stretch to reach their God-given potential. I never thought of myself as a "public speaker." I simply had to get the job done, and this was one of a number of ways I had to do it.

Even later, after I began speaking on college campuses as a way to bring academia and business together, I considered myself to be a person with an idea to sell, not a speaker whose goal was to get approval and applause.

Today, I'm a lecturer. I spend most of my time speaking to groups throughout the United States and abroad. Although I still lecture on eight college campuses a year, I do most of my work directly in the business community. I talk to boards of directors, corporate management teams, marketing groups, and industry trade associations. Since my book *The IBM Way* was published, I've also had dozens of media appearances in this country and in Europe.

All in all, I've made more than 125 public appearances during the past twelve months and will do as many during the next year. Somehow, without any planning or conscious effort on my part, my career has evolved into that of a sought-after public speaker—and I love it!

In this chapter, I'll tell you what I do in front of an audience that consistently works for me, and will work for you in your presentations and public appearances.

IT STARTS BEFORE YOU STEP ON STAGE

1. Talk only on subjects you know about. It's silly to accept a speaking engagement to talk about something that really doesn't interest you or that you have no expertise in. It happens plenty, though. About a year ago, I sat through a keynote speech sponsored by an interfaith association of churches and synagogues to open Brotherhood Week. The speaker was a local celebrity, a TV sportscaster. It took three minutes for anyone in the audience who was paying attention to realize that this guy didn't have a serious thought on the subject of brotherhood. After a prepared introduction of two or three sentences, he went into a speech about sportsmanship that he must have given a thousand times. After thirty minutes of sports anecdotes, he closed with a two- or three-sentence conclusion that included the word "brotherhood" a couple of times. The speech was a fraud. Maybe he thought he had got away with it, trying to pass off his stock speech, but he didn't. He was politely applauded, but when he offered to field questions from the floor, none were forthcoming. The audience knew he had nothing to say.

Know your subject. Stay home if you don't.

2. Know your audience. It doesn't matter whom you're speaking to—a company, a trade association, a civic or government group. Do your homework first. You want to know as much as you can about the sponsors and the group. You will feel closer to the audience if you know who they are, why they're attending (are they a captive or voluntary audience?), what they hope to get from the time they're spending with you, and anything else you can learn. It impresses and flatters them when you're able on stage to show you know something about them: their growth, structural changes, acquisitions; their successes and maybe some of their problems; whatever. It not only compliments them but draws them into your talk; it lets them know that you took your assignment seriously and that they should take you seriously. It's a speaker's way of telling the audience, "Look, I know who you are. I spent time learning about you and understanding you. I'm impressed with you. I like you." You're there because they're important. That's accomplished by tailoring the speech to their requirements and not delivering a canned talk.

3. Know exactly what response you hope to evoke. This should be thought through and determined in advance. Are you in the spotlight to motivate your audience, to rouse them, to produce or sell more, to educate, share information, raise their morale, or challenge them? You should know specifically what you want to accomplish and organize your thoughts, material, and delivery to that end.

The dynamics of the situation can sidetrack you from achieving your goal unless you have properly prepared in advance. I've delivered a lot of speeches in my life, but I listened to a lot more. I've seen successful leaders waste their own time and that of huge audiences because they apparently lost their way and forgot why they were speaking.

In preparing your speech, isolate the most important points and make sure you present them in the most dynamic and positive way possible. Don't bury them among a hodge-podge of thoughts or sandwich them between your laughs. Give them the kind of attention you'd expect from an advertising agency—that is, make sure that the most important points are distinguishable and as memorable as possible. Make sure in advance that when you and your audience separate, they will carry with them the message you intended.

4. Believe that you have something worthwhile to say. If you don't think you have anything useful to give to your audience, you will certainly feel awkward and uncomfortable and they will sense it. In maybe ninety percent of speaking situations, you will have more knowledge of the subject matter than those who are listening. In almost every case, you'll be expressing your point of view and your biases, so make sure that you are sold on the stand you are taking and are well enough prepared to present your material in the most confident, self-assured manner possible. As far as I'm concerned, what you have to communicate and how you say it are what public speaking is all about. It's the message that counts, and if it's worth presenting at all, it's worth preparing for.

WHAT KIND OF PRESENTATION
WILL WORK FOR YOU?

1. The speech that's written and read. Probably more speeches are delivered this way than any other. I understand why you might choose to read a prepared speech. It seems safe; unless you go into a total freeze, you're certain to get through the ordeal without an embarrassment or a major catastrophe. If you don't skip a page, everything you want to say will be said. And if you practice enough beforehand, you probably won't stammer or dot your presentation with too many "uh"s and nervous coughs.

To me, the reading of a prepared speech is an insult to the audience. You're set to fail the moment you approach the stage with the stack of papers in your hand. You telegraph all kinds of negatives to the audience.

One of the silent messages the speech reader transmits is: "Lord, I wish I were somewhere else." Chances are, so does the audience.

I don't think it's possible to project a comfortable demeanor or confident posture when you don't know the material well enough to present it in a more personal way.

Pull out a sheaf of papers and bury your nose in them, and the audience can lay odds that they're in for a boring time. If it doesn't turn out that way, it's a miracle. For most people, the idea of being read to for maybe an hour is appalling, and being put in a situation where you're stuck in a chair with a roomful of other uncomfortable people is nearly criminal. When I'm trapped that way, I want to shout, "Hey, I can read. Give me a copy and let me go. I'll read it at my convenience and my own pace."

I don't think that the Teleprompter is a satisfactory alternative to reading from a script. It's okay for a television speaker because the camera is panning his face, and the device keeps his head up and his eyes open. When the Teleprompter is used in an auditorium before a live audience, most speakers seem to be saying, "Hey, folks, I'm obviously reading this speech. Be good sports, and pretend that you don't notice it." For a while, a number of IBMers thought this would be a good way to improve their delivery and make it seem more spontaneous, but it didn't work. Teleprompters were set up in the first row, and the speakers read with their eyes glued on the machine, afraid they'd lose their place and miss a paragraph before they recovered their orientation. IBM management decided that the deliveries looked phony and were too stilted, so the Teleprompters were discouraged. Again, some people can use Teleprompters effectively; it all comes down to what works best for you.

A major problem with many written speeches is that they're written to be read, not to be listened to. Most people write in a more complex and compact fashion than one is used to receiving aurally. When we're reading and hit a passage that's difficult to untangle, we can reread it as often as is necessary. We can go back a paragraph or two to keep pronouns connected to their assigned nouns. We can take the time to go to the dictionary if we hit a semantic blank.

Speeches that are read to an audience tend to be stiffer, more formal, more statistical, more technical, less personal, and surely less enjoyable: less enjoyable for the reader as well as the listener.

In theatrical terms (and when you're facing an audience, it's hard not to think in these terms), this type of delivery is certain to add up to a bad show. A speech reader who faces a live audience becomes something of a talking head, forcing everyone in the room to focus on a space no greater than a ten-inch TV screen. There's little or no animation from the speaker. Gestures are unnatural and seem written into the script when it's obvious that the reader is totally committed to the written word.

It's an unpleasant, disappointing experience for everyone involved, partly because the excitement of a "live show" is lost. There's no real rapport between the speaker and the audience, and when the speech reader looks up and makes eye contact with someone in the room, it comes across as a nervous affectation.

There's a better way of presenting a prepared speech.

2. The speech that's acted. There's a big difference between standing up and reading to a roomful of people and "performing" a prepared speech. Some of the most exciting public speakers in the world deliver "canned" speeches—that is, the words are written and memorized, the gestures and movements are choreographed, and the "reader" breathes life and meaning into the script. The written word becomes a skeleton for him to flesh out with his delivery.

It's no different than the actor who brings a character to life on stage. The incredible thing about the fine actor is that the audience knows that he or she is delivering a canned speech. They know that every word, movement, action, and reaction is studied and rehearsed. They don't mind it. Why? Because the actor creates the illusion that his words are being spoken for the first time. He creates the illusion of spontaneity. His facial expressions and pauses convince the audience to "believe" that they can even see him think! They know better, but it's okay with them, even when they know the actor has performed the part a thousand times.

The acted presentation unshackles the speaker from the podium, frees him to make natural gestures, and allows him to move around. Instead of locking the audience's attention on a talking head, it broadens their viewing area, which is now limited only by the space the speaker has available.

Although the memorized, acted speech is a tremendous improvement over a speech that's read, infinitely better, there are still downsides and pitfalls to be concerned about. Like the actor in a play, you can become locked into the script; you can become so reliant that you lose flexibility and spontaneity, and that can get you in trouble. If your mind wanders for a moment and you "lose your place," you're on your own. Unlike the actor, you won't have a prompter backstage to whisper a cue, or other members of the cast to get you back on track. The audience can throw you off, by laughing in the wrong places or reacting in a way you weren't expecting. There's no room in your script for a heckler. I recommend that anyone who works this way carry a few cue cards in case something interferes with the presentation. You can learn to handle most problems on stage, and you can also protect yourself beforehand.

Think of the words you put down on paper as a *performing script*. Understand that your words, no matter how beautifully crafted, won't fly in a roomful of people unless they are specifically written to be listened to.

(a) Talk your words onto the page. Listen to them as you put them down. Write with a tape recorder at hand. Listen to what you're writing, and reject anything that doesn't sound like you, even if it's your most brilliant prose. No matter what the subject, sound conversational, informal, personal, and natural.

(b) When you write to be heard, you must avoid using

208

long, complex sentences. It's much more difficult to take in information by listening only, especially when one's in a room filled with people and there are continual sight and sound distractions.

(c) Don't worry about grammar too much; that is, don't be afraid to pepper your talk with sentence fragments, exclamations, or slang. Remember your speech isn't going to be read by the audience, and they are used to listening to fragments and other grammatical aberrations. I'm not suggesting that you throw the rulebooks away, but if you're going to be successful, you must sound natural and comfortable.

(d) Don't shy away from reiterations. Use as many examples, anecdotes, and "in other words" as are necessary to make your points. After all, you're moving on and the audience may have a tough time keeping up with you. Your reiterations will often be welcomed, because if the audience is involved, they don't want to miss any important messages.

(e) Write your speech with a vocabulary that can be understood and enjoyed by your audience. Believe me, most of what you say is going to be missed, no matter what, so don't handicap the audience by speaking in a language they don't understand or aren't comfortable with.

(f) As you write, consider the audience's response to your words. If you want to give them a few seconds to ponder a particular point, write a pause—perhaps a sip of water—into your script. Expect laughs to the humor you've included and write in the pause. We've all seen speakers and amateur actors talk right through the laughs, and then the audience has to play catch-up.

(g) About jokes: personally, I seldom include them in a lecture or any presentation, and never gratuitously or just to entertain. It's not my style, and I'd feel uncomfortable trying to do stand-up comedy. I feel uncomfortable when I'm in the

audience and the speaker tries to break the ice with a warm-up joke that you know is used in a variety of versions, depending on the group. I become embarrassed for him when he interrupts his message with, "That reminds me of the story about . . ." and tells an old joke. Put a person behind a microphone and he wants to either faint, sing, or tell a joke.

If you're really terrific at telling jokes, you may send the audience away holding their sides, but is that what you want to do? I don't think so: not if you want them to think about themselves and their performance and productivity.

I've attended lectures that were billed as "stimulating," "motivating," "thought provoking," and I left at the first opportunity because they turned out to be evenings of light entertainment—either sport figures who tried to turn a locker room pep talk into a motivational speech for business people or frustrated stand-up comics who changed the characters in their jokes to fit into the business milieu.

Hey, none of this makes me a sourpuss. I have tremendous respect for stand-up comics and think every speaker can learn a lot from them. I have nothing against bringing in a comic to entertain at a convention or at a week-long sales meeting as long as he makes a few business points; I just don't want the speaker who is responsible for motivating the audience to distract them with fictional anecdotes and old jokes.

I'm making an issue of this because so many speakers and lecturers have the mistaken idea that they are expected to be funny and search for humorous material to write into their presentations. Don't do it. It hurts a lot more than it helps.

(h) Don't leave yourself out of the script. Illustrative true stories and anecdotes make your presentation more accessible and certainly warmer and more personal. Understand that your audience will come away from your talk with more impressions than information. To them, the importance of what you say will correlate with what they feel about you, so give them a chance to know and like you.

3. The improvisation. Now let's get back to the various presentations. We covered speeches that are read to the audience and those that are memorized and "acted." You know how I feel about those that are read. There should be a law against them. The speech that's memorized, practiced, and delivered with energy and thoughtfulness can be believable and impressive. How effective it is depends on the speaker's ability to stay in character, how good he is at creating "the illusion of the first time," and how much fun he has in the role.

There's another kind of presentation, the "improvisation." It gives the illusion of being loosely structured, freewheeling, and off the cuff, but it's hardly that. The "improvisor" is really a first cousin to the stand-up comic. He's my favorite, and the kind of lecturer I strive to be. Since you already know that I seldom tell jokes, this may seem like a total contradiction, but when we go over the comic's routine, you'll see the connection. He shows up on the job with a ton of material—mostly in his head: jokes, patter, songs, and shticks. He has the bits or routines down pat. He's memorized them: practiced the intonation, the pauses, the facial expressions, the body language. He knows exactly how to handle his props: flip charts, pointer, and water glass. He's like a magician with a bagful of tricks or a singer with dozens of songs in her repertoire. He may have some new material that he hasn't mastered yet and may be anxious to give it a shot, but 99 percent of what he presents is tried, true, and reliable. Before he makes his appearance, he sizes up his audience. What he pulls from his bagful of material depends on what he discovers once he's out there.

He starts with a specific opening and finishes with a pre-

211

planned closing, but in between he's flexible, shuffling his deck when it suits him, playing with the audience—dancing, sparring, feinting, and looking for the right opening. If the audience doesn't laugh at mother-in-law jokes, you can bet he doesn't do a string of them. He feels his audience out, looks for the right buttons to push, and when he finds them, he's home free. The material flows and the time flies.

That's not exactly what I do, but it's close. What I take with me to a speaking engagement is analogous to the stand-up comic's approach. My head is filled with ideas about leadership, performance, incentives, and years of practical experience. Over the years, I've learned a lot about the corporate world: its structure, bureaucracy, and staffing. I've learned about marketing, sales, production, and communication, and dealt with tens of thousands of employees. I know that what I have to say is worthwhile. How I say it (my act, if you will) is the result of many speaking engagements, lots of practice, trial and error, editing out material that doesn't come across, and always trying to improve my delivery.

Like the stand-up comic, I plan out the opening of my talk, and I know exactly how I'll close my speech, but in between, I give myself a lot of room for flexibility. Although I know exactly what material I'll cover and which points I will hit hardest, I'm not locked into a rigid format. The order in which I present my ideas, and even the ideas I present, depend on what kind of relationship develops between the audience and me. It's partly my own sensitivity—or intuition—that guides me through the talk.

I know that the audience is not going to remember too much of what I say, and I know that what one person might consider exciting and important, another might slough off as obvious. That doesn't bother me. Although I think that everything I have to say to an audience is important, I try to showcase the four or five points I'm most anxious to have them retain. I make sure that I don't leave the stage without making those points.

So I don't write my speeches in advance. I don't have to. Throughout my career, I've been telling people what I think —selling my ideas, presenting my programs, and trying to incite others to strive for excellence. Understand that although I don't approach the stage with a prepared speech, I'm certainly prepared. I know my material and work from a mental outline; if I'm distracted or I suddenly draw a blank, I improvise, hoping that my unscheduled anecdote or news tidbit is appropriate—or at least in the ballpark.

Enough about the material; now comes the presentation.

FACING THE GROUP—ON STAGE OR AT THE SPEAKERS' TABLE

1. Are you nervous? You bet! I don't think that anyone speaks about his or her public appearances without mentioning the bouts of nervousness, or even stage fright. Like everyone else, I experience it, but I don't worry about it. That is, I don't consider it an enemy that can't be overcome. The tension begins to build even before the host starts his introduction: the edginess, the quickened heartbeat, the pang that comes with the thought that I can't remember the name of the person who's introducing me or any of my opening remarks. I quickly settle down when I hear my voice and suddenly, I have no doubts that if only one person in the room is in for a good time, it will be me!

I have no quick tips on how to alleviate nervousness. No self-hypnosis or reflex mechanism. Since I can't get rid of it, I welcome it and consider it a friend. I've convinced myself that the nervous tension that accompanies me to the spotlight keeps me from becoming complacent. It reminds me that what I'm doing is important: that I wouldn't be putting myself in a position of possible rejection if my message weren't important and people I'm addressing weren't important. The nervousness says: "Concentrate! If you don't, you'll blow it." I know this. If I didn't feel the tension, my presentation could go flat.

2. Turn up the lights. When the houselights are dimmed and I find myself separated from the audience by a row of footlights, I feel physically removed from the people I want to reach. Zap a spotlight on me and I feel as isolated as if I were speaking in a vacuum. That doesn't happen to me anymore, because I insist that the houselights be on, so I can see the audience as clearly as they can see me. I need the closeness. My remarks become more like a conversation when I can see whether or not my words are hitting or missing the mark, and I can react immediately to the messages sent back. It's the one way I draw the audience into my talk. They know that their presence is important to me and that I feed off their energy and interest.

Anyone who has ever spent time in front of a group of people knows the exhilarating difference between an audience that's with you—one that's charging the atmosphere with its energy and interest—and the audience that seems to say, "Okay, I'm here—so entertain me."

I look into the eyes of the people in the audience, as many as I can. Not everyone agrees on that point. Some teachers and

214

coaches suggest that speakers simply give the impression of looking into the eyes of their listeners. "Look over their heads," they say. "It's not as distracting for you and it will make them feel close to you anyway."

Maybe so, and it might work for you, but it doesn't work for me. I need to make honest-to-God connections. After a talk, I can tell what dozens of people look like and what they were wearing. The greatest compliment after a talk is when someone says, "I thought you were talking just to me."

3. Project confidence and enthusiasm. I've listened to presentations that embarrassed me for the speaker. Some were given to small groups (maybe a board of directors), others in auditoriums filled with conference-weary salespeople. It was their self-conscious, humble why-in-the-world-are-you-listening-to-me attitude that was so off-base. You must do everything you can to feel secure before you begin. Of course, know your material and know you can present it in an interesting and, better yet, engrossing way. Make sure that you look all right: your hair, shoes, and clothes. Take care of as many details as possible. Are your props in place, notes in order, lights the way you want them, microphone on and volume adjusted, zippers zipped? If you're an after-dinner speaker, don't eat too much and don't drink at all. You want to be in total control of yourself: no slow reactions, slurs, or other unpleasant surprises.

Never open your speech with an apology. When I hear someone say, "Please bear with me. I, uh, didn't have much time to prepare for this talk, you see . . ." I want to pick up and leave. Always project confidence, never discomfort. Many times, I've been one of several speakers on a program, and more than once, I've followed some of the more popular speakers in America onto the platform. Lee Iacocca, Charles Kuralt, and Bill Cosby come to mind. I've had to wait until the thunderous applause died down before I could begin, but I never

215

did what so many speakers do when they follow a powerhouse speaker; I never opened with something like: "Wow, what an act to follow! (Ha-ha.) I wish I could come back tomorrow. (Ha-ha.) Wasn't he great?" Instead, I do what I always do. I thank the introducer, give the audience and myself a few moments to look each other over, and begin my talk as though everybody in that room were there only to hear what I had to say. And I do my best to convince them that there's no place in the world I'd rather be right at this moment. I'm there to influence them in one way or another, right? If I want them to think what I think, do what I suggest, or become excited because I'm excited, I'm sure as hell not going to present myself as a negative. They are going to know from the outset that I am confident, comfortable, and enthusiastic.

If you know and respect your material, and if you make up your mind that you are going to have a good time presenting it, your delivery will be fine. But here are a few random tips that you might find helpful:

(a) Try not to stay behind the lectern. It's a strain on the audience to keep their eyes focused on one spot, and it limits the vitality you can project. And don't hang onto it with a death grip or drape your body over it; it's unprofessional and distracting.

(b) Don't be tentative about your movements. When you pussyfoot around the stage, you look self-conscious. All your movements should seem purposeful. If you want to move upstage (away from the audience), don't take small backward steps. Turn away from them. Take your steps, then turn back.

Don't walk away from the audience when you're talking. Hold your line until you've made your move and are facing them again.

Little hand and arm movements come across as awkward and jerky. Gestures should be broad and graceful.

Eliminate as many nervous habits as possible. They can be deadly distractions on stage. I know a fellow who stood in front of his audience with both hands jammed in his pockets. One hand held coins and the other his key ring; and his fingers never stopped moving. It looked as if there were a couple of live frogs in his pockets. I was so distracted by the action under the blue serge that I missed huge chunks of his presentation, and I'm sure everyone else did too.

Paper clip straighteners drive me up a wall. These people usually speak in conference rooms with their papers spread before them. Before they're done, they've managed to mangle a few clips and distract those who were close enough to focus on their finger dexterity.

(c) Make certain that you can be heard. Check out the microphone in advance of the presentation. If you are being put in a position where you must speak frequently, take a speech course. Even the smallest voice can be helped with a little training.

Incidentally, a good presentation can be ruined when a speaker with a hearty voice continually shouts into a microphone and there's no one controlling the sound level electronically. You must be conscious of the volume that's being projected into the room. If it's too low, you can lull the audience to sleep. If it's too loud, the audience may suffer physical discomfort. Neither is what you want. If you're uncertain how your voice is projecting, ask the audience.

(d) Don't talk too fast. What's too fast? When you rush your lines so quickly that the audience has to strain to keep up with you, and when the words run together, slurred; also, when the tone of your voice becomes higher than usual and you can feel that your throat is tight, not relaxed and open.

Some speakers, wanting to put emotion in their voice, speed up; the tone is raised and the effect misses its mark.

(e) Put variety in your delivery, but don't rush it. Slow down by pausing between thoughts. Let the audience see a thought develop. Use your props.

Speed up, not by running one thought into another but by shortening your vowels and popping your consonants. You can drive a point home by talking either louder or softer. Do both.

Variety! It keeps the audience alert and interested: variety in tone, volume, length of sentences, and movements.

(f) Let the audience know what kind of reaction you expect as your presentation unfolds. You do it by your own actions. A broad smile, a clenched fist, a pointing finger, arms stretched to heaven, or whatever is comfortable for you. Come to think of it, anything that you'd like to do will feel comfortable if you practice it enough.

(g) Underscore your most important points by gesture and tone. Somehow you have to telegraph to the audience that although everything you have to say is important, some things are more important! Your delivery must work like a yellow highlighter on a gray printed page.

(h) Watch the clock. Don't run over your allotted time, even if you sense that the audience is truly enjoying your talk and you're having a ball. Though I know what time it is, I want the audience to know that I'm watching it; so I always look at my watch twice during every presentation. Thus they know that I respect their schedule and won't run over. Actually, I try to close a few minutes early. It's much better when someone

218

says, "I wish he would have talked longer," than the opposite comment.

(i) Screen out as many problems as you can, but maintain your poise when the unexpected occurs. In order to keep the headaches down to a minimum, I check out the facility before I'm scheduled to speak. Besides gaining a "feel" for the place and getting comfortable, I make sure the lights, microphones, and PA system are in working order. It's good to know in advance if the air conditioner is operating and whether or not it's a noise hazard. No matter how careful you are, if you speak frequently, you will run into aggravations that can drive you up a wall. Don't let them get to you. Stay calm and cool and you'll survive the date and even triumph. Once I was about ten minutes into a speech when lightning struck the power plant and plunged the room into total darkness. In a split second, I had the battery-operated mike in my hand, and when the crowd realized I was going on with my talk, they stayed in their seats. The power was out for more than thirty minutes and when the lights finally came on, I was completing my final remarks. From the lively question-and-answer period that followed, I got the message that the audience had really appreciated that I was willing to make the best of a bad situation and they in turn had made a greater than usual effort to concentrate on the talk and get as involved as possible.

People ask my advice on handling hecklers or unexpected disturbances in the audience. Since the turbulent '60s, when every "establishment" speaker was harassed on college campuses, I haven't had any serious problems and only a couple of minor ones. I can only tell you this. No matter what the disturbance (someone who drinks too much at the banquet that precedes your talk or someone who angrily disagrees with a point you made), try to handle it as dispassionately and with as much dignity as possible. It's a mistake to try to heckle the heckler. I'd get no pleasure nor accomplish anything worthwhile by embarrassing a loudmouth in front of a roomful of people. If someone wants to make a point, I firmly but pleasantly promise him the opportunity after I've completed my presentation and the question-and-answer session has begun. Don't let anyone pull you out of your planned routine. Don't let anyone cause you to change the tone and tempo of your presentation.

(j) About question-and-answer sessions after your talk: Don't invite or submit to them if you don't know your material well enough to field challenging questions. You may deliver a great prepared speech and then come off as shallow, because you faked an answer or got confused by the question. If you don't know the answer, then say so!

Personally, I look forward to the Q & A sessions. They're very important. One, they're a way to get an immediate reaction to your presentation. (The applause might be misleading.) Two, they allow you to correct some mistaken impressions and fill in some gaps. But most important, they give you the opportunity to get closer to your audience: to draw them into your presentation and, in a sense, share the spotlight with them.

To me, delivering a speech—that is, facing a live audience with the purpose of influencing a change in its attitude or behavior—is the most exciting and challenging communication vehicle of all. The dynamics are so different from selling your ideas one-on-one, whether it's across a desk or by a letter or memo. It's an adventure and a special kind of challenge to try to push the right buttons and exact the desired response from a diverse group of people.

The greatest challenge of the public-speaking experience, and its biggest frustration, comes from the fact that much of your message, no matter how eloquently presented, will be lost on the audience. Some estimate that perhaps eighty percent of the data presented are not retained and not retrieved unless your talk is supported with handouts that can be studied afterward.

That means that the "music," not the "lyrics," in your presentation may be the most important factor in conveying your message. It's safe to assume that the impression you make with your tone, enthusiasm, sincerity, self-confidence, and style will do more to motivate and influence the audience than your statistics, data, and beautiful prose.

13

Finally ...

Although I've spent my adult life working in a world of high technology, I fervently believe that it will be people, not machines, that save this country from drowning in a sea of mediocrity. Silicon chips, lasers, robots, and artificial intelligences can't assure us our position as a great industrial nation that can excite its people and sit at the top of world commerce. Government can't do it, not by protectionism or revision of the tax structure or any other legislation. Acquisitions and super-mergers aren't the answer, either.

I hope you agree with me that the weaknesses we have to deal with in this country are rooted in people and that these problems must be addressed at every level of our society, beginning with you and me. I'm not being hysterical or theatrical when I insist that we declare war on those things that have contributed to the enervation of this nation: indifference, complacency, cynicism, rejection of the work ethic, and drug and alcohol abuse.

As individuals, we have to reject mediocrity on all fronts; we must expect quality workmanship and excellent service. We must demand that we get our money's worth and settle for nothing less.

We must not tolerate rudeness or abuse in any shape or

form from anyone, whether we work for him or he works for us.

We must do everything we can to bring an end to the drug and alcohol abuse epidemic by attacking the problem head-on in the workplace as well as at home. We must let our co-workers know that we do not want to work with people whose performance is impaired or sub par. If we're in positions of leadership, we must implement strong policies that will keep mediocrity out of the workplace. We must not allow ourselves, wittingly or unwittingly, to add to or nurture the condition that has this nation dragging its feet.

Individually, we must keep complacency out of our personal lives and strive to give our very best performance, day in, day out: reaching for new heights and stretching to maximize our potential.

That doesn't mean becoming a workaholic and giving everything you have to a job or profession. Workaholics sometimes produce impressive results but are not my role models. More often than not, they're disorganized, insecure, obsessive. No, doing the very best you can rarely means doing the most you can, and it never means doing more than you can do well. Maximizing your potential and doing your very best consistently requires attending to the many details I've covered in these pages, so I'll close this book by reviewing a few.

- Get on good terms with yourself. Build yourself up physically, mentally, and emotionally.
- Nurture your self-esteem. Believe that you are important and that your performance at home and on the job makes a difference.
- Know what you want to accomplish.
- Understand the importance of prioritizing your goals, short term and long term, and developing strategies for attaining them.

- Acquire and maintain the skills, knowledge, and tools needed to do your best.
- Understand that people, not jobs or industries, are exciting and creative, just as people, not their work, may be dull and boring.
- Understand the importance of the way you're perceived, and conscientiously project the image you desire, and live up to.
- Be cognizant of the effect you have on others: how you influence their ideas, behavior, and feelings. Use the power to uplift the environment wherever you are: its mood, its energy level, and its intensity.
- Never lose sight of your values and beliefs. Make them part of your daily life. Think about them, articulate them, demonstrate them to your friends, family, colleagues, and to everyone else you come in contact with.
- Never stop teaching.
- Never stop learning.

There's no magic in an individual's greatness or in a company's. There are countless ways of attaining greatness, but any road to reaching one's maximum potential must be built on a bedrock of respect for the individual, a complete commitment to excellence, and a total rejection of mediocrity.